STRATEGIC BALANCE IN THE INDO-PACIFIC REGION: CHALLENGES AND PROSPECTS

STRATEGIC BALANCE IN THE INDO-PACIFIC REGION: CHALLENGES AND PROSPECTS

Editors

Cdr MH Rajesh

Dr Raj Kumar Sharma

(Established 1870)

United Service Institution of India

New Delhi

Vij Books India Pvt Ltd

New Delhi (India)

Published by

Vij Books India Pvt Ltd
(Publishers, Distributors & Importers)
2/19, Ansari Road
Delhi – 110 002
Phones: 91-11-43596460, 91-11-47340674
Fax: 91-11-47340674
e-mail: vijbooks@rediffmail.com

ISBN: 978-93-86457-28-8 (Hardback)

ISBN: 978-93-86457-29-5 (ebook)

Contents

Participants

Vice Admiral Satish Soni, PVSM, AVSM, NM (Retd)

Vice Admiral Satish Soni, PVSM, AVSM, NM (Retd) was the Flag officer Commanding-in-Chief Eastern Naval Command. Before this appointment, he was also the Flag officer Commanding-in-Chief Southern Naval Command.

Vice Admiral Satish Soni is an alumnus of the National Defence Academy and was commissioned into the Indian Navy on 01 July 1976. A specialist in Navigation and Aircraft Direction, the Flag Officer is an alumnus of the Defence Services Staff College, Wellington and College of Naval Warfare, Mumbai.

Vice Admiral Satish Soni has held various important command and staff appointments in his career. The Flag Officer's sea commands include the ocean going minesweeper Kakinada, the guided missile corvette Kirpan, the guided missile frigate Talwar and the guided missile destroyer Delhi. He has had the honour of having commissioned two warships, Kakinada and Talwar, in Russia, as the Commanding Officer. His staff appointments include Deputy Director of Personnel, Joint Director of Naval Plans and Naval Assistant to Chief of the Naval Staff at IHQ MoD Navy).

On his elevation to Flag rank, Vice Admiral Satish Soni assumed responsibilities as the Assistant Chief of Personnel (Human Resource Development) at IHQ MoD (Navy). Subsequently, the Flag Officer commanded the Eastern Fleet of the Indian Navy, and thereafter took over as Chief of Staff, Eastern Naval Command. Vice Admiral Satish then followed it by being appointed as Commandant, National Defence Academy at Khadakvasla, Pune. In his previous assignment, the Vice Admiral served as Deputy Chief of the Naval Staff at Integrated Headquarters MOD (Navy) at New Delhi.

Lt Gen P K Singh, PVSM, AVSM (Retd)

Lt Gen P K Singh was commissioned as a 2/Lt in the Indian Army in 1967. He retired as an Army Commander (C-in-C) in 2008. He is a graduate of the Defence Services Staff College, Wellington; the Higher Command Course and the National Defence College. His academic qualifications include MSc; MPhil and Post-graduate Diploma in Business Management.

He took over as Director of the United Service Institution of India in January 2009. The General is a member of the Governing Council of the Indian Council of World Affairs, New Delhi, and also the International Advisory Board of the RUSI International, London.

Vice Admiral Arun Kumar Singh, PVSM, AVSM, NM (Retd)

Vice Admiral Arun Kumar Singh retired in 2007, as FOC-in-C (ENC). During his 40 year career, he commanded various warships, submarines, submarine bases and submarine squadrons. A specialist conventional submariner and navigator, he was trained in the former USSR in nuclear submarines and missiles. He is an alumnus of the Indian DSSC, NWC, NDC and the Russian Admiral Makarov Academy. As a Commodore he served in NHQ as Director of Tactics and Director of Submarine Operations. After promotion to Rear Admiral in 1996, he held the double hatted appointments of Flag Officer Submarines and Assistant Chief of Naval Staff (Submarines), and later was appointed Flag Officer Commanding Eastern Fleet, when he exercised with most navies of IPR including China and Japan. In 2003, he was promoted to Vice Admiral and held the following appointments. He was the DG of the Indian Coast Guard. In this capacity he signed the Hotline Agreement in 2005, with the MSA of Pakistan, and also exercised with the Coast Guards of Japan, South Korea, Maldives and Sri Lankan Navy. He also commanded the Indian Coast Guard rescue and relief operations in India, Sri Lanka and Maldives, after the Tsunami disaster of 26 December 2004. As DGICG he was also Chairman of the National Maritime Search & Rescue Board, Chairman of National Oil Spill Disaster Contingency Plan, Chairman Offshore Security Committee and was member Board of Directors of Goa Shipyard. He was C-in-C of the Andaman Nicobar Command and FOC-in-C, Eastern Naval Command.

Post retirement the Admiral worked in the private shipbuilding sector for 4 ½ years and was also involved in Track 2 talks for 4 years. Presently, he is a council member of the USI, NMF and member of the IDSA. He is a prolific writer and speaker on issues maritime, nuclear, international affairs, and has addressed various institutions in India and abroad.

Lt Gen MollahFazle Akbar (Retd)

Lt Gen Mollah Fazle Akbar, ndc, psc was commissioned in the Corps of Artillery, Bangladesh Army on 30 November 1976. His last assignment was Commandant, National Defence College (NDC), Bangladesh prior to superannuation in February 2016. Presently he is working as Advisor of Regent Airways, Bangladesh operating in domestic and international routes. He is also The Chairman of Board of Directors of a Financial Institute, Bangladesh Industrial Finance Company Limited (BIFC).

In his long service career, he served as the Brigade Major of two Infantry Brigades, Staff Officer in Directorate General of Forces Intelligence (DGFI), Grade One Staff Officer (Training & Operations) in an Infantry Division, Assistant Defence Adviser at Bangladesh High Commission in India and Colonel Staff in an Infantry Division. He also performed as Director of Military Operations and Director of Artillery in General Staff Branch, Army Headquarters.

Lt Gen Akbar commanded an Air Defence Artillery Unit. He also commanded the only Air Defence Artillery Brigade (ADA) of Bangladesh Army and a Field Artillery Brigade. He also commanded a Sector of the then Bangladesh Rifles, present Border Guard Bangladesh (BGB). He was also a Sector Commander of UN Peace Keeping Force in UNMIL (United Nations Mission in Liberia). Before his current assignment at NDC he was the Chief of Defence Intelligence of Bangladesh as the Directorate General of Forces Intelligence (DGFI).

He attended Anti-Aircraft Firing Drone Course from China and Security Intelligence Administration Course from United Kingdom. He earned his Masters of Philosophy (M.Phil.) from National University of Bangladesh.

Post retirement, the General is an active participant at International Seminars & Conferences and presents papers on contemporary issues.

Dr Changsu Kim

Dr Changsu Kim is an eminent journalist, author and strategic thinker, currently a Senior Research Fellow with the Center for Security and Strategy at the Korea Institute for Defence Analyses (KIDA) in Seoul, Korea. Prior to serving as the Director of the institute from February 2012 till January 2014, he headed numerous divisions viz. Japan Studies Division, Regional Military Affairs Division, US Studies Division and the Division of International Conflict Studies. He was also the Director of the Center for Security and Strategy. He was also an APSA Congressional Fellow with the Office of Rep. Solomon P. Ortiz (D-TX), 1989-90.

Dr Kim graduated from the Hankuk University of Foreign Studies in Seoul in 1977 and received his MA and PhD in Political Science from the University of Cincinnati in 1981 and 1985, respectively. He has been the Editor-in-Chief of The Korean Journal of Defence Analysis (KJDA), a quarterly English journal registered with the SSCI. Besides authoring numerous KIDA reports and English books and articles on the ROK-US alliance and the USFK, he has written extensively on subjects of US Defence and military strategies, Northeast Asian Security Affairs, ROK-US-Japan trilateral security cooperation, and multilateral security cooperation on WMDs and transnational threats.

He was the Special Assistant to the Minister for Policy at the ROK Ministry of National Defence and also a NIDS Fellow at the National Institute for Defence Studies, Tokyo, Japan. For the last 8 years, he has been a member of the Planning and Coordination Committee of the National Unification Advisory Committee, a blue-ribbon Constitutional organization that advises the President of the ROK on unification issues.

Dr Kim has to his credit immense contribution as a participant in many international security and defence forums, including the Shangri-La Dialogue, the Xiangshan Dialogue, and the Seoul Defence Dialogue (SDD), an annual track 1.5 dialogue hosted by the ROK Ministry of National Defence.

Lt Col Ngo Thanh Tung

Lt. Col Ngo Thanh Tung was born in August 16, 1975 in Ha Noi. He enlisted in the Army in 1993 after graduating from high school. He was a cadet in Military Foreign Languages College from 1994 to 1998 and

College of Military-Political Officers from 1998 to 2001. Then, he worked in Institute for Defence International Relations (IDIR) as an researcher of ASEAN-ARF Division, Deputy Head of Asia-Africa Division, Deputy Head of America Europe Division. In July, 2016, he was appointed as Head of Asia-Africa Division of IDIR and holds this position until now.

Lt. Col Ngo Thanh Tung has passed training courses abroad such as UN Military Observer Course, Australia, Jul-Aug, 2008; Maritime Security Course, April, India, 2009; Advanced Security Cooperation Course in APCSS, Hawaii, US, Jun-Jul, 2011; Joint Military Operations Staff Course in National Defence University, China, Sep-Nov, 2013. He has also participated regional defence meetings, defence cooperative activities and workshops on regional security issues.

Senior Colonel Mu Changlin (Retd)

Sr Col Mu is Senior Research Fellow at China Institute for International Strategic Studies which he joined in 2012, after superannuation from the Army. Born in Jilin Province of China in 1956, he was commissioned into the PLA in 1972 where he served successively as Company Commander, Battalion Commander, Staff Officer, Section Chief and Deputy Director of Bureau at the Ministry of National Defence (MND).

His overseas experiences include tenures as a UN Military Observer in Western Sahara, Deputy Defence Attaché in Chinese Embassy in the UK, Army Representative of the Chinese Delegation to the UN Military Staff Committee, and Defence Attaché in Chinese Embassy in Israel. He holds a Master's Degree in International Politics.

Maj Gen RPS Bhadauria, VSM (Retd)

Maj Gen RPS Bhadauria is a Distinguished Fellow at United Service Institution of India,New Delhi. He regularly conducts strategic gaming exercises for the war colleges of the Indian Armed Forces and Indian Foreign Service Institute. He retired from the faculty of National Defence College, New Delhi in Feb 2016 after serving in the Indian Army for 36 years.

The General has commanded a Mountain Division and Brigade and has vast experience in anti-terrorist operations, both at policy formulation and execution levels. He holds a Master of Philosophy Degree in National

Security and Strategic Studies from Madras University, India, and has attended a course on Politics and Strategic Affairs at Escola Superior de Guerra in Brazil.

Post retirement from the Indian Army, the General is actively pursuing his deep interest in research and writing on the security environment in Indo Pacific region, particularly South Asia.

Ms Sumitha Narayanan Kutty

Ms Sumitha Narayan Kutty, a journalist by profession, is currently an Associate Research Fellow at the S Rajaratnam School of International Studies (RSIS), Singapore. She started her career as a reporter with Times Now, Mumbai in 2007 before joining the Georgetown Journal of International Affairs, Washington, USA in 2011. Thereafter she has been a researcher with the Atlantic Council of the United States, Washington and also with the Takshashila Institution, Bengaluru prior to her current assignment.

An extremely bright student, Ms Sumitha was a university rank holder during her BA in Journalism from Mangalore University and her thesis while pursuing her PG Diploma in Broadcast Journalism from Asian College of journalism, Chennai was adjudged the 'Best Dissertation'. She later went on to complete her Masters in Security Studies from Georgetown University, Washington USA. She is fluent in Hindi, Malayalam, Tamil, and also communicates reasonably well in Persian and Arabic.

Her research work centers on security and foreign affairs with focus on South Asia and the Middle East and has been published in prestigious journals such as The Washington Quarterly, Asia Policy. She also has to her credit, interviews on her work by Bloomberg, CNBC and Channel News Asia, as also professional commentaries in The Diplomat, Business Standard, The National Interest, Ai-Monitor and Lawfare.

Dr Victor Sumsky

Dr. Victor Sumsky is the Director of ASEAN Centre in MGIMO University, MFA of Russia. His three monographs and many articles are mostly dedicated to political histories and present day development of Southeast Asian nations, international relations in East Asia and its security problems.

Prior to this assignment, he has worked for the Soviet Foreign Ministry, Institute of Oriental Studies and Institute of World Economy and International Relations (IMEMO) in Moscow. He has done extensive research, and he lectures at the University of Philippines, London School of Economics, and the University of Washington. Dr. Sumsky represented Russia on the Board of the European Association of Southeast Asian Studies (EuroSEAS) from 2004 to 2010. As a member of CSCAP, Russia he regularly contributes to the activities of CSCAP Steering Committee and study groups, and speaks at its General Assemblies. His Op-Eds and commentaries appear in printed and electronic media, both in Russia and abroad.

Among Dr. Sumsky's numerous awards are the Medal of the Order of Friendship (Vietnam, 2014) and the Medal of the Order of Merit for the Motherland, 2nd grade (Russia, 2016).

Ambassador Veena Sikri, IFS (Retd)

Veena Sikri's has been India's High Commissioner to Bangladesh and Malaysia, India's Consul General in Hong Kong, and Director General of the Indian Council for Cultural Relations (ICCR), New Delhi (1989-92). She has held challenging and prestigious assignments at the Indian Embassies in Moscow, Kathmandu, Paris, and at the Permanent Mission of India to the UN in New York, where she represented India in the UN Security Council, and at Summit meetings of the Non-Aligned Movement (NAM).

After retiring from Government, Veena Sikri joined academia in 2009 as Professor; Ford Foundation endowed Chair, Academy of International Studies, Jamia Millia Islamia University, New Delhi. She was concurrently Visiting Senior Research Fellow with the Institute of South East Asian Studies (ISEAS), Singapore. Her work at ISEAS resulted in a book: "India & Malaysia: Intertwined Strands" (2013).

Veena Sikri is the Founder and Convener of SWAN (South Asia Women's Network), launched in March 2009 at Jamia Millia Islamia. With its unique focus on gender empowerment as the key to sustainable economic growth, social development and environmental sustainability in South Asia, SWAN brings together women leaders from nine South Asian countries: Afghanistan, Bangladesh, Bhutan, India, Maldives, Myanmar,

Nepal, Pakistan and Sri Lanka. Professor Veena Sikri is Vice Chairperson of the South Asia Foundation (India Chapter), a secular, non-profit and non-political organization, with eight autonomous chapters across South Asia.

Professor Yang Minghong

Professor Yang Minghong is currently the Executive Director of the Faculty of Social Development and Western China Studies at Sichuan University. His educational background includes Bachelor's and Master's degrees in History from Sichuan University, a doctorate from Sichuan University and post-doctoral work at the South-western University of Finance and Economics.

His research areas include Tibetan studies, macroeconomics & social development, South Asian studies and agricultural economics and management. He has a number of published articles to his credit. His extensive work covering regional economics, borderlands studies, Tibet development, and exiled-Tibetans is widely respected among international academia.

Ms Shebonti Ray Dadwal

Shebonti Ray Dadwal is a Senior Fellow with the Institute for Defence Studies and Analyses (IDSA), heading the Non-Traditional Security Centre at the Institute. She is also a member of the Editorial Board of IDSA's flagship journal Strategic Analysis. Prior to joining IDSA, she served as Deputy Secretary at the National Security Council Secretariat and was Senior Editor with The Financial Express. She is also a member of the CSCAP Study Group on Energy Security as well as member of the Core Group on Myanmar of the MEA's Indian Council of World Affairs (ICWA).

Her research focus is on Energy Security and has recently published a monograph on The Geopolitics of America's Energy Independence: Implications for China, India and the Global Energy Market. She has written two books. The first, Rethinking Energy Security in India was published in 2002, while the second one, Geopolitics of Gas: Implications for India is ready for publication. Apart from writing several peer-reviewed articles and papers focusing on Energy Security, she has also co-edited and co-authored the book Non-Traditional Security Challenges in Asia:

Approaches and Responses, (Routledge ;2015), and the IDSA Report on Security Implications of Climate Change for India (2009), respectively.

In April 2009, she was awarded a Chevening Fellowship by the Foreign and Commonwealth Office of the UK on completion of a course in Economics of Energy at the Institute for Energy Research and Policy, University of Birmingham, UK.

Dr Huang Yunsong

Professor Huang Yunsong is an Associate Professor in the Faculty of Social Development and Western China Development Studies at Sichuan University. His educational background includes Bachelor's and Master's degrees in Law from Sichuan University, a doctorate from Sichuan University and post-doctoral work at the University of Michigan.

His research areas include Public International Law, International Studies, South Asian Studies and Refugee and Asylum Law. He has a number of published articles to his credit and has pioneered the understanding of some critical issues in China-India relations such as the exiled Tibetans in India and the Indo-China border dispute.

Ambassador Sanjay Singh, IFS (Retd)

Ambassador Sanjay Singh is an alumnus of Delhi University, from where obtained a Master's degree in Physics. He joined the Indian Foreign Service in 1976 and served in Indian Missions in Mexico, Germany, Ghana and France as also in the Ministry of External Affairs, New Delhi. He was Director in the Office of the External Affairs Minister and Joint Secretary and Head of Division dealing with Latin American Countries. From October 1997 to June 2001, he was India's Consul General in Ho Chi Minh City and from July 2001 to August 2004, Deputy Chief of Mission in Paris. He held charge in the Ministry as Joint Secretary and Additional Secretary (Gulf) from March 2005 to March 2009. He was India's Ambassador to Iran from March 2009 to March 2011. He took over as Secretary (East) in the Ministry of External Affairs in March 2011 and retired in end April 2013.

Admiral (Dr) Jayanath Colombage (Retd)

Admiral (Dr) Jayanath Colombage is a former chief of Sri Lanka Navy. Highly decorated for both gallantry as well as distinguished service, he served the Sri Lanka navy for the entire spectrum of war with the LTTE. During a career spanning 37 years, he commanded various ships and four naval areas.

The Admiral is a graduate of Defence Services Staff College in India, and Royal College of Defence Studies, Asia Pacific Center Security Studies (USA) and holds a PhD from General Sir John Kotelawala Defence University (Sri Lanka). His doctoral thesis; 'Asymmetric Warfare at sea: The Case of Sri Lanka' has been published by Lambert Academic Publishing, Germany. He also holds Master's degrees in Defence and Strategic Studies from Madras University as well as International Studies from Kings College, London.

He is a maritime security specialist &practitioner; he has rich experience in countering maritime terrorism. He has presented and published papers on maritime security, IUU fishing, blue ocean economy, combatting global terrorism and extremism including maritime terrorism in various local and international forums. His work titled 'Maritime Security and Theories of Naval Warfare; Way ahead for a professional Navy' at the International Research Conference, Kotalawela Defence University was adjudged the 'Best Paper' in 2015. Certified by the IMO as a lecturer on International Ships and Port Facility Security (ISPS) Code, Admiral Colambage is a visiting lecturer at Defence Services Command and Staff College (Sri Lanka), Kotelawala Defence University and also a fellow of Nautical Institute, London UK.

Currently, he is the Chairman of Nautical Institute Sri Lanka Branch. He was formerly Chairman of Sri Lanka Shipping Corporation and an adviser to the President of Sri Lanka on maritime affairs.

Dr Mohammad Jasim Uddin

Dr MD Jasim Uddin is a Research fellow at BIISS, Dhaka since 2009. Prior to this he has been a research officer with the same institute and also the National Institute of Local Government, Dhaka, Bangladesh. He is also the Assistant Editor of the prestigious BIISS Journal and a life member of the Bangladesh Economic Association.

A PhD from the Jahangirnagar University, Dhaka, Dr Jasim Uddin also holds Master's Degrees from University of Antwerp, Belgium and Islamic University, Kushtia, Bangladesh. He also has a Bachelor's Degree in Economics.

He is a prolific writer who has to his credit, a number of publications and articles on a diverse range of subjects such as South Asian security, economic development, international relations and the Global War on terror. He is also a regular participant at national & international seminars on these subjects.

Vice Adm Shekhar Sinha, PVSM, AVSM, NM** (Retd)

Vice Admiral Shekhar Sinha retired two years ago as the Flag Officer Commanding in Chief (FOC-in-C), Western Naval Command after four decades in the Navy. He was Chief of Integrated Defence Staff at the MoD prior to taking over as FOC-in-C. US Global Bussiness Forum has honoured him as distinguished veteran.

A naval aviator from the fighter stream, he has the unique distinction of being the only pilot to have flown from the deck of all three carriers India has had. He has held command of four ships including the missile destroyer INS Delhi, two air squadrons and the Naval Air Station, Goa. His other important assignments include Fleet Operations Officer and later Fleet Commander of the Western Fleet, Flag Officer Naval Aviation and Goa Naval Area, Assistant Chief Of Naval Staff (Air), Controller of Personnel Services and Deputy Chief of Integrated Defence Staff (Operations and Perspective Plan & Force Development). He was instrumental in obtaining the first ever approval of the Tri services Long Term Integrated Perspective Plan by the Government of India.

A graduate of Defence Services Staff College, College of Naval Warfare and the National Defence College, Admiral Sinha is a recipient of PVSM and AVSM. He has also been awarded the Nao Sena Medal twice for gallantry at sea.

Presently he is a security and strategic analyst. He mentors Cyber Security Consortium in Delhi.

Ambassador Gleb Aleksandrovitch Ivashentsov

Ambassador Gleb Aleksandrovitch Ivashentsov is the Deputy Head of the Russian Center for APEC Studies with the diplomatic rank of Ambassador Extraordinary and Plenipotentiary. He graduated in 1967 from the International Economic Relations Faculty, Moscow State Institute of International Relations, and in 1991 from the Russian Diplomatic Academy. A polyglot, he can read Russian, English and Hindi and fluently speaks German and French.

During his long and illustrious career, he has been Consul General of USSR/ Russia in Bombay from 1991-1995, Ambassador of Russia to Myanmar from 1997-2001 and Ambassador of Russia to the Republic of Korea from 2005-2009.

Ambassador Ivashentsov has been conferred state awards, namely 'The Order of Friendship' (Russia) in 2003 and 'Khanhwa Medal for diplomatic merits' (Republic of Korea) in 2009.

He has a number of acclaimed publications to his credit. His most recent publications in Russian are India – Basics in Brief (2009) and Behind the Fortifications of 38th Parallel (2012). In the Korean language, he has authored The Other Korea (Seoul, 2012) and in English, The Tiger of the Land of Morning Calm (New Delhi, 2014). He has also been Special Research Fellow at the China Center for Contemporary World Studies.

Ms Kristy Tsun-Tzu Hsu

Kristy Hsu (徐遵慈) is Associate Research Fellow and Section Chief at the Taiwan WTO Center and Programme Coordinator at the Taiwan ASEAN Studies Center (TASC), Chung Hua Institution for Economic Research (CIER), Taiwan (R.O.C.). Her areas of research include international trade policy and economic & trade law, trade & development issues, regional integration and gender issues.

She is also Advisory Member to the Trade and Development Committee, ROC National Confederation of Industries, International Affairs Committee, ROC Chamber of Commerce, and adviser to the Chinese National Association of Industry and Commerce monthly publication, CNAIC Magazine, and Standing Supervisor to Taiwan Women Film & Video Association.

Kristy obtained her LL.M from the School of Law, Soochow University, Taiwan, and B.A. in Foreign Literature and Languages from National Taiwan University, Taiwan. She was the Executive Secretary and associate research fellow at the Chinese Taipei APEC Study Center, Taiwan Institute of Economic Research (TIER) from 1999 ~ 2002; journalist of the Commercial Times in Taiwan from 1989 ~ 1998, and Correspondent in Tokyo for the newspaper in 1990.

Maj Gen (Dr) Nguyen Hong Quan

Maj Gen Nguyen Hong Quan is Deputy Director General of Vietnam Institute for Defence Strategy (IDS). During his service, Major General Nguyen Hong Quan has tenanted prestigious command, instructional and staff appointments, notably, Deputy Director General of the Ministry of National Defence Foreign Relations Department (FRD). He was also a United Nations Observer in Algeria in 1997.

The General has attended several overseas courses, the notable ones being courses at the International Institute of Public Administration (IIAP, France) and at the Institute for Higher Studies of National Defence, France (IHEDN). Apart from that, he is an alumni of the Diplomacy College, holds an M.A from the Diplomatic Academy of Vietnam and a Ph.D. in World History from Hanoi National University's Social Sciences and Humanities Division. He is also a graduate of Vietnam National Defence Academy (NDA).

He is an active participant in prominent international seminars and conferences, has authored three books and published over 150 articles and opinion pieces in domestic and foreign academic and professional journals.

Dr Christian Wagner

Christian Wagner is Senior Fellow at the German Institute for International and Security Affairs (SWP), Berlin. His main areas of research are India and South Asia with a focus on foreign policy and security issues. In 2015, he was a visiting fellow at the Observer Research Foundation (ORF) and at the Jawaharlal Nehru Institute for Advanced Studies (JNIAS) in New Delhi.

Cmde Lalit Kapur (Retd)

Commissioned into the Indian Navy in 1975, Cmde Lalit Kapur is a specialist in Navigation and Aircraft Direction. He was a member of the Fifth Indian Scientific Expedition to Antarctica where he pioneered a technique for survey of the Ice Shelf in the vicinity of Dakshin Gangotri.

The Commodore has served on a variety of Western and Russian origin ships, including command of a squadron of Ocean Minesweepers and INS Vikrant. An alumnus of DSSC, Wellington and CDM Secunderabad, he has been part of the faculty at both these institutions as well as at the College of Naval Warfare, Mumbai. He was Defence Adviser, Embassy of India, Muscat, with concurrent accreditation to the UAE, Qatar and Bahrain. Other experience includes being part of the founding team of India's Defence Intelligence Agency, heading its Protocol and Foreign Liaison Division; heading the Systems and Sea Vector Branches in the Strategic Forces Command; and heading the Operations Division at Headquarters Offshore Defence Advisory Group, Mumbai.

Commodore Lalit Kapur has a number of published articles on international relations, military history and maritime issues to his credit.

Maj Gen BK Sharma, AVSM, SM** (Retd)

Bal Krishan Sharma, AVSM, SM** (Retd), the Deputy Director Research and Head of Center for Strategic Studies and Simulation at United Service Institution of India (USI), New Delhi. He specialises in Strategic Net Assessments, Scenario Building and Gaming. He conducts strategic games for the National Defence Collage, Higher Command Course of the Army, Navy and Airforce and Academy of India Foreign Service, New Delhi. He has edited Books and "Strategic Perspective", digital magazine for USI of India and also written articles in Indian Foreign Journals on strategic affairs. He regularly delivers lectures at premium military and academic Institutions in India and abroad. He regularly participates in International Conferences as well.

Introduction

Lieutenant General PK Singh, PVSM, AVSM (Retd)

Strategic Balance in the Indo-Pacific Region: Challenges and Prospects

The Indo-Pacific Region is combination of the Asia Pacific Region (APR) and the Indian Ocean Region (IOR) connected by the busy straits of Malacca, Sunda and Lombok. The region encompasses almost half of the world population, a third of the top twenty economies, world GDP and exports. It is home to an enormously populous and diverse mix of ethnicities, cultures, political systems, religions and economies. As a confluence of two busy oceans, the region is the maritime highway of the world that combines emerging markets and resources of Asia and Africa with rest of the world. China benefits immensely from the existing international system and yet is not content with its west-centricity. China strives to create its own version of security and economic architecture.

The Indo Pacific Region is the center of gravity of global power shift. While the US seeks to maintain a status quo in the world order and international system, China, on the other hand, asserts for recognition as a major power and strives to carve out its own sphere of influence. Russia, Japan, South Korea, India and the ASEAN countries have become important stakeholders in the balance of power in the Indo Pacific Region and pursue their core objectives through dynamic balancing of interests. Contestation over maritime territories has led to military build up to protect perceived core interests. These are manifest in China's building military infrastructure over disputed islands/shoals/reefs, US assertions for freedom of navigation through the disputed waters, militarization of maritime space, stand offs in the ADIZs and nuclear brinkmanship by North Korea. The region now faces far more virulent form of collusive hybrid threats that combine asymmetric conflicts with conventional wars, under a nuclear overhang. The whole region is highly susceptible to terrorism, proliferation of radical ideologies, cyber-crimes, nuclear terrorism, piracy and multitude of international crime. Environmental degradation, calamities and pandemics pose an even bigger challenge to the humanitarian security. Blue Economy, has gained traction for sustainable management of oceans. Democracy, delivers a stake to billions in the region. The security environment in the Indo Pacific is impeding the promising economic potential of the region-which some call a paradox.

Indo Pacific Region is the epicentre of global economy in terms of availability of natural resources, trade flow and transportation of energy over the Western and the Eastern SLOCS to the West, East Asia and South Asia. The countries of the region are members of emerging economic architectures such as TPP, RCEP, Asia Infrastructure Investment Bank, BRICS bank etc. China's Belt and Road Initiative, India's Projects; Mausam, Spice route, Sagar Mala and ASEAN's economic dynamism, add new dimensions to the nature of economic competition and cooperation. The economic heft of Indo Pacific Region lies in the competing economic blocs such as TPP and RCEP. The TPP would have a combined GDP of $ 26 trillion i.e., about 40 per cent of global GDP and over 30 percent of world exports whereas, the RCEP includes more than 3 billion people, has a combined GDP of about $17 trillion, and accounts for about 40 percent of world trade.

The strategic environment in the Indo Pacific Region is characterized by myriad of security risks. The existing security architecture in the Western Pacific and initiatives such as 'Declaration of Parties' and 'Code of Conduct' have proved ineffectual in mitigating security challenges and fostering cooperative security or building strategic trust. Likewise, the security paradox in South Asia needs a 'de novo' approach to break away from the prevailing Zero Sum narrative. There is a need to review and harmonize the functioning of regional organizations in Asia Pacific like– the APEC, ARF, EAS, SCO, SAARC, GCC, IORA and IONS. Integration of regional economies within and outside the region will lead to co-prosperity in a win-win paradigm. How can the emerging economic architectures such as TPP, RCEP, 'Belt and Road Initiative' be made more inclusive, merits informed debates. The IOR is gaining economic and security salience. There are no well – established security and economic architectures in the IOR. How should we initiate a strategic dialogue to build collective security, energize economic integration and build trans-continental economic and security linkages? The seminar seeks to provide a platform for cross-fertilization of views to build peace and promote prosperity in the Indo Pacific Region in a win-win paradigm.

This book is based on the papers presented by various speakers at the 37th USI National Security Seminar on the theme of, **"Strategic Balance in the Indo-Pacific Region: Challenges and Prospects"** held 03 and 04 November 2016 at New Delhi. The seminar brought together varying perspectives on security challenges, mapping of economic potential and proposing architectures for collective security and economic integration. The USI, since 2009, has been hosting an international seminar every November to look at the issues in the Indo-Pacific Region. This year's seminar was held in the background of heightened tensions in the Western Pacific which needless to say will have effects in Indo-Pacific and its impact will be felt globally over a long period of time. The aim of the seminar was to have a free and fair exchange of ideas in a cordial environment.

The keynote address by Vice Admiral Satish Soni set the tone of the seminar where, as a practitioner of security, he gave an overview of the Challenges and Prospects in Strategic Balance in the Indo-Pacific Region. He described the strategic contours of the Indo Pacific, assessing the various key actors in the region such as India, China and the United States of America. The keynote address also touched upon an emerging area like Blue Economy. He summed up by saying that US, India, Japan and China have a predominant role to play in ensuring that the region remains stable. He attributed the limited success of present institutional arrangements to divergent approaches and competing national interests. He suggested creation of effective institutional mechanisms both for promoting collective economic benefits and countering common security threats through greater people-to-people and Navy to Navy contacts. The seminar that followed was organized into three separate sessions.

The first session covered 'Security Challenges and Prospects in the Indo-Pacific Region' and was chaired by Vice Admiral AK Singh (Retd) with Lt Gen MF Akbar (Retd), from Bangladesh, being the co-chair. During the session six speakers from various countries presented their papers focussing on 'Maritime Disputes in the East China Sea and their

Implications for Regional Security'; 'an overview of geopolitics of the East Sea disputes and its implications for regional stability'; 'China's Perspective on the Maritime Disputes in the Western Pacific'; 'Dynamics of Indo-Pak and Sino-India Border Disputes and its Implications on Stability of South Asia'; 'The Islamic State's Influence in the Indo-Pacific Region'; and finally on 'Non-Traditional Security Challenges in the Indo-Pacific Region: Prospects for Cooperation'.

The second session, devoted to 'Economic Challenges and Prospects', was chaired by Ambassador Veena Sikri, IFS (Retd) while the co-chair was Prof Yang Minghong from China. The session had five speakers covering 'Geopolitics of Energy Resources in the Indo-Pacific Region'; 'China's Belt and Road Initiative - Challenges and Prospects'; 'Perspectives on other Emerging Economic, Infrastructure and Trade Corridors in the Indo-Pacific'; 'Blue Economy and Coastal Management in the Coming Decade'; and 'Challenges to Regional Economic Integration in Indian Ocean Region - Way Forward'.

The concluding session focussed on 'Emerging Architecture in the Indo-Pacific Region: Way Forward'. The session was chaired and co-chaired by Vice Admiral Shekhar Sinha (Retd) and Ambassador Gleb A. Ivashentsov from Russia respectively. Four papers were presented covering, 'A Prognosis of Competing Economic Architecture in the Indo-Pacific Region (RCEP, TPP and other Economic Institutions): Way Forward; 'Confidence Building Measures and Evolution of Security Architecture in the Western Pacific'; and 'Security Architecture in the Indian Ocean Region: Way Forward'.

Each session was followed by an open house discussion among the participants and the audience. Important issues raised during these discussions have been summarised in the conclusion. We hope proceedings of the seminar will help develop a nuanced understanding of existing and emerging challenges and help us provide inputs to policy makers, scholars and researchers for future research.

Keynote Address

Vice Admiral Satish Soni, PVSM, AVSM, NM (Retd)

Introduction

It is indeed an honour and a privilege to be invited to deliver the Keynote address at this annual International seminar organised by the USI. At the outset, I must compliment the USI for the yeoman service they continue to render as a think tank of the Defence Services. Of special significance is the quarterly journal, the oldest defence publication in Asia, which the USI publishes since 1871. The Institution owes much to the vision and scholarship of Col Pyare Lal who nurtured it from 1957 to 1987 as its secretary. I would like to take this opportunity to compliment Lt Gen PK Singh, Maj Gen Sandhu and the staff of USI who have lived up to his legacy and continued to provide impetus to the endeavours of this institute. Young officers in the field who are far removed from the humdrum of discussions on strategic issues benefit immensely from the distilled analysis in your quarterly journal and other publications.

During the last four years of my service, I have tenanted the appointments of Flag Officer Commanding in Chief of the Eastern and Southern Naval Commands. During my tenures, I travelled to most of the countries of the Indian Ocean Region, ASEAN, China and Japan and got an opportunity to interact with the senior leadership of the host Navies. My views, therefore are those of a practitioner rather than an academic.

Seminar

The broad theme of the seminar is familiar - indeed, strategic balance in the Indo-Pacific region is a subject that is being studied and researched by several think tanks. However, I must acknowledge that USI has done well by planning individual sessions in a very comprehensive manner and we will be able to hear speakers from different parts of the world covering a variety of issues ranging from maritime disputes to Blue Economy. What may perhaps be a first is the presentation of a paper on the influence of the Islamic State in Indo Pacific. Whilst the content of the presentations are essentially the views of individual scholars, it would not be wrong to assume that the official positions are not much at variance. So, this is an excellent opportunity to network, exchange views, allay misunderstandings and discuss solutions to the many vexing issues.

Indo Pacific

Oceans have always been significant geostrategic spaces and very often a stage for competition and rivalry amongst resident power structures. The Indo-Pacific is no different. In addition to the traditional rivalries on account of Maritime disputes, there has been a rise of non-traditional threats such as terrorism, piracy, drug trafficking, climate change and the need to provide security to Blue Economy initiatives. The nature of these security challenges in the region has serious implications for the entire sea faring community and requires an international cooperative response. The Indian Ocean has been relatively stable though US Naval ships have had minor skirmishes with the Houthi rebels off Yemen and with Iranian Patrol boats in the Persian Gulf but I would like to highlight a somewhat different challenge; that of dealing with a nuclear armed state with a propensity to sponsor terrorism. The attempted hijack of a warship in 2014 is indicative of the fact that the use of nuclear weapons by terrorists at sea is no longer in the realm of fiction.

However, the situation in the Western Pacific region is becoming very complex. The region is experiencing a wave of Maritime assertiveness as indicated by development of infrastructure on disputed islands and territories, unilateral declaration of Air Defence Identification Zones, nationalisation of disputed islands, a distinct hardening of stance in Defence White Papers, forays of navies into distant waters, strident reactions to EEZ transgressions - perceived or otherwise, reinterpretation of the constitution, enhancement of naval capabilities including procurement of submarines and expeditionary platforms, challenging of the widely accepted rule of law by outright rejection of the judgement of the PCA, use of fishing militia to assert sovereignty and so on.

There has also been a marked increase in levels of maritime cooperation – by way of bilateral and multilateral summits, exchange of arms and defence technology, joint naval exercises, staff talks, port visits and visits by Service officers. For example, the Rim of the Pacific Exercise off Hawaii in August 2016 saw participation by 45 ships, six submarines, 200 aircraft and 25000 personnel from 26 countries; the Malabar exercise has progressively increased in terms of its scope and complexity with Japan being included in the 2016 edition; and there have been several 'firsts' in terms of bilateral naval exercises, the ones between India and Australia, and India and Indonesia that were held recently, being examples. Nations are striving hard to provide maritime security to their people.

Let's look at the major players.

United States - The Predominant Player

Post Second World War, the United States of America has been the predominant power both in the Indian Ocean and the Pacific. PACOM, CENTCOM and now AFRICOM, a host of naval bases, military units stationed across the oceans and strong alliances have helped US maintain an edge over others. As the geostrategic significance of the Indo-Pacific region has rapidly increased, the US believes that its interests would be best served by a rebalance to the East. The 'Pivot' is a comprehensive strategy which aims to protect and promote American economic, geostrategic and military interests in the region by strengthening diplomatic and military engagements with its traditional allies and emerging partners. However, the US strategy appears to be still evolving and while the US still remains the most powerful country in the world in terms of its military and economic power, there are important questions and doubts arising on its commitment, given the US involvement in Syria and the extent to which it is able to go to protect its allies in case of a major conflict. China is clearly unhappy with the American pivot to the East as it perceives it to be an attempt to contain China. Most regional allies and partners welcome the US pivot, which they believe would help in balancing China's growing economic and military assertions in the region. At the same time, they seek to constructively engage with rising China, which they consider important for the region's overall peace and prosperity. Moreover, it would be impractical to keep a rising China isolated in an era of increasing economic interdependence. As seen by the pronouncements by President Duterte of the Philippines,

America's regional allies and emerging partners may be beginning to doubt its ability to provide support in decisive situations.

Resurgent Maritime Powers - India and China

Historically, Oceans have largely been unregulated and to some extent remain so even today. They however have contributed immensely to the growth of world economy especially in the last century. This progress could be achieved because unarmed merchant marine could transit the waters and discharge their cargoes to the destinations safely. During the last century, security to the merchant marine has largely been provided by the western navies - British and the US being the major contributors. Equations are however changing and China and India are emerging as the resurgent powers. The Western navies including the US are shrinking if not declining; so, who's capable of taking over the mantle of ensuring Maritime Security of the global commons? Let me give you a brief historical perspective of the two main players who may influence the strategic balance in the Indo-Pacific: namely, India and China.

India

The strategic location of the Indian Peninsula made it a focal point for trade, maritime activity and international relations for centuries. Buddhist texts dating back to 600 BC mention navigation in the Bay of Bengal and Indian Ocean by Indian mariners, especially from the Coromandel Coast to Sri Lanka, Burma and South East Asia. During the rule of the Kalingasbetween 300 to 150 BC, several maritime expeditions were dispatched to Sri Lanka, Indonesia, Myanmar, China and Japan, resulting in the spread of Buddhism. During the tenth and eleventh centuries, the Chola Dynasty traded actively with Indonesia,Cambodia, Malaysia and China. Unfortunately, India lost touch with the seas in the 12th Century, became captive to a continental mind-set, and consequently, suffered the self-inflicted poverty of a landlocked state. It was no surprise that when a new naval power, Portugal, entered the Indian Ocean, it faced no credible opposition whatsoever.

China

The Chinese too have a similar maritime history. Earliest references to maritime trade date back to 722 to 481 BC and from 960 AD onwards, they consolidated naval power with maritime trade peaking during 1405 to 1433 AD; The signature initiative being the famous voyages of the legendary Chinese Admiral Zheng He. Incidentally he died in Kerala as also Vasco da Gama much later. Chinese influence on the Malabar Coast is evident in the use of the famous Chinese nets in Kochi even today. Threats from land set in a similar continental mind-set and the Chinese declined as a maritime nation, eventually experiencing a century of humiliation from 1840s to 1940s when they were invaded from the sea repeatedly and forced into signing unequal treaties with the English and the Japanese.

Evidently, history has taught both countries a lesson- if their increased maritime orientation these days is of any indication. However, both would do well, to constantly remind themselves that the world expects them to contribute to maritime security and not jeopardise it.

I will discuss India and the Indian Ocean first.

The Indian Navy considers itself as a net provider of security for the smaller countries of the Indian Ocean Littoral and has been actively engaged in capacity and capability building of the regional Navies. Our ships are deployed for EEZ surveillance missions in friendly countries that have a large Exclusive Economic Zone, but lack the wherewithal to patrol it. We train over 800 foreign personnel in our institutions every year. Ships, aircraft, equipment and spares have been given gratis to several friendly countries, a recent example being a Fast Attack Craft gifted to Seychelles in October 2015. Friendly navies use our dockyards for refitting their ships. Our survey ships are also deployed regularly to other countries, for carrying out hydrographic survey in their waters. The Indian Navy has taken the initial steps to bolster Maritime Domain Awareness in the IOR by commissioning Coastal AIS stations, a Coastal Radar Chain, a NC3I network and setting up an Information Management and Analysis Centre (IMAC) in Gurgaon which collates inputs from different sources and disseminates them to the security agencies. The Indian Navy has also helped other smaller island countries in the region to improve surveillance by setting up AIS chains and Coastal Radar stations. A bold initiative to share White Shipping Data (from Africa's East Coast to beyond Malacca) with 29 countries has been proposed, with 11 countries already concluding this agreement with India. Our long standing maritime boundary dispute with Bangladesh has been settled by a UN Arbitration Tribunal recently. It may not have been entirely in our favour; however, what is important is that we have accepted it and the two nations can now move beyond the issue. We routinely exercise with the navies of USA, Russia, UK, France, South Africa, Singapore, China, Australia, Japan, Malaysia, Indonesia, Cambodia and South Korea. The Indian Navy has been carrying out coordinated patrols with Indonesia and Thailand for a few years now, and has recently started similar patrols with Myanmar. Staff Talks are held regularly, wherein, apart from ongoing initiatives, additional avenues for cooperation with other navies are also explored.

In sum, our relationships in the Maritime arena are robust.

Now a few words about China and the South China Sea

China has a coastline of 18000 kms, a 11 trillion dollar economy… expected to be a 17 trillion economy in near future, a per capita of 9000 dollars, a defence budget of 200 billion dollars expected to grow to 400 billion. Some analysts put the Chinese over the US in more than one areas - GDP in PPP terms, exports, foreign exchange reserves, ship building, turnover of ports to name a few. If there is any country which ought to be keen for a stable Maritime order, it is China, more so because of the dependence on the five trillion trade which passes through the South China Sea annually.

China's claim on the South China Sea by promulgation of the famous nine dash line in 1948, exercising jurisdiction over the Paracel group of islands, establishing the Sansha City on Woody island in 2012, the Scarborough shoal incident in Apr 2012, declaration of an Air Defence Identification Zone over the East China Sea in Nov 2013, reclamation of 3200 acres on seven features in the Spratly group of islands and the outright rejection of the verdict by the Permanent Court of Arbitration on South China Sea has made countries of the region somewhat insecure. Some are strident; others are biding their time. The Chinese proposal of stitching a Maritime Silk Road has met a cautious response as sceptics are not entirely convinced about the benign nature of this proposal, primarily because of its opaque nature. A visible manifestation of the PLA Navy's modernisation is the increased deployment of Chinese ships and submarines in the Indian Ocean. These actions are indicative of abandoning the traditional continental mind-set, and shifting focus from offshore waters to open seas protection as has been emphasised in the latest Chinese Defence White Paper. Though China's rise has benefitted regional countries in the economic field, its increasing expenditure on military modernization and power projection, particularly in the East and South China Seas, have caused some concerns for them and the US.

What do we do to allay misunderstandings? How do we ensure that a rule based maritime order is enforced? And most importantly who lays down the rules? These are some of the questions before the intelligentsia here.

While geopolitics and geostrategic issues are the flavour of the contemporary strategic discourse, two important issues merit attention. These will soon form part of the security discourse i.e. Blue Economy and Sustainable Development Goals 2030.

Blue Economy

Nearly seventy two percent of the earth's surface is covered by oceans and seas, much of which is either under explored or unexploited. The oceans and seas are both an engine for global economic growth and a key source of food security. Countries are looking to the seas for economic prosperity, food security and social wellbeing of their people, and there is a growing realisation that the emerging construct of Blue Economy holds great significance especially for the Indian Ocean Rim Region which is home to nearly one-third of the world's population. The rising demand for seabed minerals such as polymetallic nodules, polymetallic sulphides and cobalt crusts has resulted in increased commercial interest in seabed minerals. A term often heard in this regard is the 'new gold rush'.

On Sep 27, 2015, the global community announced commitment to Sustainable Development Goals 2030 in which Goal 14 is to 'Conserve and sustainably use the oceans, seas and marine resources for sustainable development'. There is a symbiotic relationship between Blue Economy, Sustainable Development Goals (SDG) and Security and therefore ocean governance has become critical to ensure safety and security of economic assets and activities such as offshore oil platforms, protection of marine wealth, prevention of illegal fishing, and upholding national environmental regulations thereby ensuring livelihoods of coastal populations as also enforcing national commitments to international agreements and initiatives such as the SDG 2030.

The need to provide maritime security to ocean resources is going to be the next challenge for all of us.

Conclusion

There are a number of challenges that we will need to overcome for striking a strategic balance in the Indo-Pacific region. In my opinion, US, India, Japan and China have a predominant role to play in ensuring that the region remains stable. Present institutional arrangements appear to have limited success because of divergent approaches and competing national interests. The big challenge before us therefore to create effective institutional mechanisms both for promoting collective economic benefits and countering common security threats. There is a need for acceptable multilateral frameworks for building strong architectures that enforce a rule based order. Greater people-to-people and Navy to Navy contacts through an institutionalized approach will help in promoting overall peace, security and prosperity in the region, which is our common goal. I am certain that with the experts present here, we will certainly be able to collate recommendations for our respective governments to follow.

I wish your deliberations all success and once again thank the USI for organizing this seminar and inviting me to attend it.

PART – I

Security Challenges and Prospects in the Indo-Pacific Region

Maritime Disputes in the East China Sea and Their Implications for Regional Security

Changsu KIM

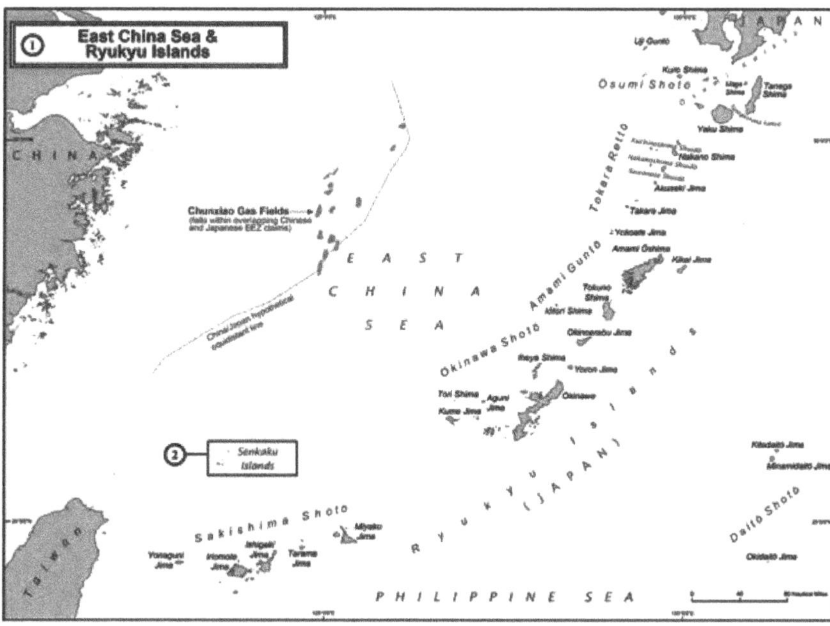

Source: U.S. DoD, Asia-Pacific Maritime Security Strategy, 2015, p. 9.

Maritime Disputes in the East China Sea: Historical Backdrop

A glance into the chronology of major maritime incidents and disputes in the East China Sea between Japan and China helps us understand the origin and a tenacious nature of the competing power rivalry in East Asia over small islands, rocks and gas fields. To be precise, these maritime incidents and disputes are a microcosm of how Japan and China, Taiwan and the U.S. have managed their international relations in that part of the world for more than 120 years. Indeed, these countries have differing and increasingly conflicting national interests, security and military strategies in regard to their maritime disputes. In their domestic politics, the highly visible maritime incidents and disputes are often reflective of the very complicated and multifaceted aspects of their public opinions—humiliation, historical grievances, new-found national pride and nationalism, and a growing sense of urgency to restore the Old Glory, and even a sort of irredentism. In other words, these maritime incidents and disputes have many different dimensions, including History, Law, Security, Psychology, and Public Opinion. The ongoing maritime incidents and disputes in the South and East China Seas cannot and should not be focused merely on the legal and military aspects of freedom of navigation and overflight. What concerns us more here at the USI national security seminar is that they are reflective of their national strategies to enhance as well as to reduce threats to their territorial integrity, sovereignty, security, and power positions. Important historical details in this regard are:

1372, 1403, 1534: China, in retrospect, claims ownership based on some old written records on Diaoyutai in the context of the Ryukyu Kingdom.

1879: Japan incorporates the Ryukyu Kingdom and renames it as Okinawa Prefecture.

1894: Japan conducts surveys on Uotsuri-shima and other islands.

1895: Japan unilaterally annexes five uninhabited islands (*terra nullius*) and three barren rocks in the East China Sea, calls them "Senkakus." China's Qing Dynasty cedes Taiwan and adjacent islands to Japan under the Treaty of Shimonoseki, ending the First Sino-Japanese War. The Senkaku Islands are not included in the treaty.

1945: Japan surrenders, ending WWI, and returns Taiwan and adjacent islands to China in accordance with the Cairo Proclamation (17 November 1943) and Potsdam Proclamation defining Terms for Japanese Surrender (26 July 1945). The U.S. military takes control of the Okinawas and Senkaku Islands.

1951: WWII officially ends in Asia under the Treaty of San Francisco which is "deliberately ambiguous about the ownerships of islands and reefs in the

East and South China Seas," resulting in the current Japan-China standoff.

1969: A UN report says studies suggest the presence of large oil reserves in the waters of the Senkaku islands

1971: Taiwan, China officially claim sovereignty over the Senkaku Islands, calling them Diaoyutai and Diaoyudao, respectively. The U.S. confirms Japan's "residual sovereignty."

1972: Japan regains control of the Okinawa/Ryukyu Island Chain, which includes the Senkaku Islands from the U.S. with the signing of the Okinawa Reversion Treaty.

2005: A Taiwanese boat protests near Okinawa.

2008: Japan and China reach a principled consensus on joint development of resources.

2010: Japanese Coast Guard ships collide with a Chinese trawler. The Chinese captain is detained for two weeks in September, resulting in suspending political and cultural exchanges and stopping rare earth exports to Japan.

2012: Japan purchases and nationalizes three islands (September), prompting large-scale protests and pro-China activists sailing and swimming ashore and Japanese nationalists landing on Uotsuri-shima to assert Japan's sovereignty. Also, Chinese ships and planes enter Japanese-controlled waters and airspace, citing overlapping jurisdictional claims.

2013: China declares "East China Sea Air Defence Identification Zone" (23 Nov)

2015: China builds several new drilling platforms on its side of the median line. (since mid-2013).

2016: Japan sets a radar system on one of its oil platforms and Chinese Coast Guard vessels and fishing boats challenge Japan's territorial claims on the islands. China also deploys a radar system on a Japanese oil platform, violating the spirit of a 2008 agreement on joint development of resources.[1]

1 See Over the Line: Tracking Energy Competition in the East China Sea, 14 October 2016.

Positions of the claimants and other relevant countries

Japanese position

Japan claims that during the period of 1895 to 1927, as many as 247 Japanese of 99 Koga families lived on Uotsuri, Minami, Kita and Kuba islands. Before this period, the tiny islands had long remained uninhabited. Since 1972 when the Ryukus/Okinawas were returned from the US occupying forces, Japan has exercised effective control over the Senkaku Islands. Therefore, Japan maintains that there has been no territorial dispute with China over the islands per se, but only maritime incidents involving fishing boats, patrol boats, law enforcement ships and, more recently, naval vessels in their continuous waters and maritime standoffs over oil and gas reserves and fishing rights on the high seas in the northern East China Sea. In the words of recently appointed minister of Defence Tomomi Inada's, these coercive attempts and unprecedented moves by China clearly represent "China's unprovoked escalation in the waters surrounding Japan and its attempt to change the status quo."[2]

The 2010 New Defence Planning Guidelines codified the issue of strengthening the Defence of Japan's south western island chain including the militarization of the western most island of Yonaguni. After a referendum for the residents of the island was passed on 22 February 2016, the Japanese government implemented its old plan to deploy a surveillance force on Yonaguni, long after a resolution was adopted in 2008. An estimated 150 JGSDF personnel reportedly operate a set of surveillance systems and a radar station to monitor Chinese maritime and air activities around the disputed islands in the East China Sea.

The 2013 National Security Strategy (NSS), the subsequent revised National Defence Program Guidelines (NDPG) and the Mid-Term Defence Program (FY2014-FY2018), and the new Japan-U.S. Defence Cooperation Guidelines of 2015 emphasize the creation of a "Dynamic Joint Defence Force," in which southwestern theaters, maritime-air operations, and preparations for 'grey zone' contingencies including that of the Senkakus were given higher priorities.[3] The JSDF will be engaged in collective self-Defence with the U.S. forces to defend the Senkakus.

2 Inada speech on the Evolving Japan-U.S. Alliance Keeping Asia-Pacific Peaceful and Prosperous at CSIS, Washington, DC, 19 September 2016.

3 See Hiroshi Yamazoe, "Japan's Newer Steps in its Evolving Security Policy,"

Japan has criticized China's four oil rigging structures including Chunxiaotian/Shirakaba Field and Tianwaitian/Kashi Field and 12 other structures (including 2 jackets only) in the East China Sea as clear evidence of an "attempt to set in place a new status quo for the region, an approach that has points in common with Chinese land reclamation operations in the South China Sea."[4] These new activities by China are viewed as part of China's dream of building a strong maritime power, in the name of exploiting marine resources.

Chinese position

In recent years China has challenged other claimants and relevant countries in the vast South China Sea by constructing seven or eight artificial islands in the Nansha (Spratly) Islands and three in the Xisha (Paracel) Islands with air strips, military facilities and structures in order to, among other things, safeguard their territorial waters and Exclusive Economic Zones. However, China has challenged Japan, Taiwan and the U.S. in understandably different ways in the East China Sea. While China has obviously tried to bring connectivity to the East China Sea from the South China Sea, the two Seas have some distinctive characteristics in terms of history, topography, geo-space, and potential utility. It would be difficult to draw an inference from China's position on the South China Sea, which can be seen in the following speech, to learn about its position on the East China Sea:[5]

> China has built an oceanic survey station for the UN on the Yongshu Jiao and started the construction of two multifunctional lighthouses on the Huayang Jiao and Chigua Jiao, and these construction projects are for the purpose of providing international public service...these construction projects fall well within the scope of China's sovereignty and are legitimate, justified and reasonable. They do not target any other countries or affect the freedom of navigation. There are no changes in China's claims in the South China Sea, no changes in China's position on peaceful resolution of the relevant disputes through negotiation and consultation, no changes in China's will to safeguard the freedom and safety of navigation in the South China

Chapter 11, NIDS Joint Research Series (No. 14), 7 September 2016.

4 *NIDSEast Asian Strategic Review 2016*, The Japan Times, 2016, p. 116.

5 Speech by Adm. Sun Jianguo, Deputy Chief of Joint Staff at the 2015 Asian Security Summit (a.k.a. Shangri-La Dialogue) in Singapore.

Sea, and no changes in China's goal to uphold peace and stability in the South China Sea. We hope relevant countries will work together in the same direction to build the South China Sea into a sea of peace, friendship and cooperation."

Rather, China's position on maritime disputes in the East China Sea can be and should be understood from a fundamentally different angle. For China, they are primarily the legacy of domination by the Western and Japanese Imperialism over a declining Qing Dynasty China. The centuries of humiliation imposed by foreign powers should give way to the rise of an economic and military strong power of China. This sense of containment and rivalry with Japan and the United States in its surrounding waters has prompted the Chinese leadership to develop a vision of a strong maritime power with a new maritime strategy, reorganization of its force structure, building and acquisition of advanced naval and air force weapons and equipment plus cutting-edge strategic assets, and most importantly increases in Defence budgets. All these efforts by China boil down to its aim to enhance and extend its A2/AD capabilities.

Also, the East China Sea is extremely important to China's broader security, which faces rapidly growing energy demands for oil and gas on its path to an advanced nation. It is likely that China will demand its own version of freedom of navigation and overflight around the Diaoyu as it has been challenged in the South China Sea by the United States and its allies and partners. The November 2013 declaration of its own ADIZ over a large swath of international airspace over the East China Sea including the Diaoyu Islands and gas fields[6]was Beijing's response out of these considerations.

Taiwan's position

With respect to the maritime disputes in the South China Sea, Taiwan made it clear that it cannot and will accept the ruling of the PCA, because of its implications for the Taiping Island, which is under effective control of Taiwan.

6 China claims jurisdiction based on the natural prolongation of its continental shelf and a 200 nm EEZ, whereas Japan claims an EEZ as a median line that bisects the East China Sea.

With respect to the Senkaku/Diaoyu dispute, Taiwan has long claimed its ownership over the Diaoyutai, for reasons of history and geographical proximity. While Taiwan has maintained good security relations with Japan and China, it has many commonalities with the Mainland China in terms of the maritime disputes over the island. Depending on the Cross-Strait relations, Taiwan may have to change its position on these maritime disputes with Japan.

Also, Taiwan has criticized the recent JGSDF deployment in Yonaguni as a sign of re-emerging Japanese militarism. Taiwan says that it needs a "calm and quiet air and naval training space to strengthen its Defence," while Japan needs an intact and straight ADIZ line to cover its territory without asking Taiwan to make concession on its ADIZ line.[7]

U.S. position

The United States has no official position on which country owns this tiny archipelago, but is committed to the Defence of Japan in case of any military conflict with China. That is, the U.S.-Japan Mutual Defence Treaty covers the Senkakus, which fall into the sphere of treaty obligations. For example, U.S. Secretary of State Hillary Clinton in a meeting with her Japanese counterpart Seiji Maehara in September 2010 declared her country's full support for Japan's position on the Senkaku Islands, citing Article 5 of their Defence treaty. This position has been echoed and reiterated in all subsequent meetings and moves, such as the Amendment to the FY 2014 Defence Authorization Act, the April 2014 Summit between Obama and Abe in Tokyo, the April 2015 "2+2 Ministerial Meeting" and the Obama-Abe Summit in Washington, and the new U.S.-Japan Defence Cooperation Guidelines of 2015. The United States has openly committed to its treaty obligation to defend the Senkaku Islands as part of its Asia-Pacific Maritime Security Strategy,[8] in recognition of the fact that Japan has the administrative supervision over the Senkaku Islands, because the islands belong to Okinawa Prefecture's administrative supervision.

7 Tiehlin Yen, "The Yonaguni Referendum and its Implications for Future East Asian Security," *Prospects and Perspectives 2015*, Prospect Foundation, March 2016, p. 32.

8 U.S. Depart of Defense, *Asia-Pacific Maritime Security Strategy*, August 2015. The Report maintains the need to maintain regional security order in the Asia-Pacific by all countries concerned.

It is worth noting that the three objectives of the U.S. DoD in the Asia-Pacific region can be all applied to the East China Sea: to safeguard the Freedom of the Seas (for economic and security reasons); to deter conflict and coercion; and to promote adherence to international law and standards.[9]

From the U.S. perspectives, the Senkaku Islands are located at a critical strategic point in the Rebalance Strategy of the Obama Administration and will continue to be so in the next administration. The U.S. position appears to hold an assertive China in check and to maintain the rules-based international order. And, to this end, the U.S. has maintained close relations with its allies and partners—Japan, South Korea, Australia, the Philippines, Thailand, Singapore and India.

Evolving Strategic Balance in the East China Sea

Faced with Chinese challenges over the Senkaku Islands, oil and gas fields, and other interests in the East China Sea as a whole, Japan has been a clear and strong proponent of the U.S. Navy's FON operations in the South China Sea, but has said it has no plan to participate. Rather, Japan wants to have joint maritime exercises with coastal countries and use the South China Sea as a transit in its efforts to protect SLOCs and to block China's ambition to gain hegemony via the sea.[10] Japan has been pressed to strengthen and deepen its security arrangements with the United States and to expand security cooperation with many regional countries in its competition with China over these current and latent maritime clashes in the East China Sea. Japan has made bold diplomatic and economic outreaches to many countries in the Asia-Pacific as the cornerstone and linchpin of the U.S. pivot and rebalance strategy in the region.

Japan's maritime power has been assessed as stronger than that of China in terms of power projection, logistic support, and joint military operation. To be sure, China has been at a disadvantage over high-sea

9 Freedom of the Seas means all of the rights, freedoms, and lawful uses of the sea and airspace, including for military ships and aircraft, recognized under international law. Ibid., p.2.

10 See Hideaki Kaneda, "The Xi Jinping Administration's Quest for Maritime Hegemony," *AJISS- Commentary*, No. 231, 13 July 2016. The author proposes that Japan deter and contain China with the three arrows of a stronger defense, deeper alliances, and regional coalitions.

operations. But China has strengthened and expanded its naval power in recent years to counter these weaknesses relative to Japan. In other words, China has made remarkable modernization efforts to catch up with Japan, abridging the gap between the two navies in the East China Sea. China's dream of becoming a strong maritime power has been manifested in its renewed emphasis on building power projection capabilities in their surrounding seas including the East China Sea.[11]

Also, in contrast with Japan, China has defied and protested against what it sees as the clear U.S.-led strategy to suppress and contain its rising economic and military power. The perception has fed its frenzy over the oppositions and protests by other regional powers in the South China Sea over China's land reclamations and construction of military structures, for example. China has not backed down, but rather boosted its A2/AD capabilities, primarily to counter military interventions by the U.S. and its allies and partners within its First and Second Island Chains, in the name of the Rebalance to the Asia-Pacific. The U.S. takes this Chinese military strategy as threatening its power projection by countering its naval presence and surveillance operations, and by targeting its allies in the South China Sea and East China Sea.[12]

The U.S. has apparently sought to counter China's increasing A2/AD capabilities. The Pentagon developed an Air-Sea Battle (ASB) concept, which was later developed into "Joint Concept for Access and Maneuver in the Global Commons," which aims, in Beijing's view, to neutralize its capability to defend its home waters. This trend will likely continue under the next U.S. administration. A recent CSIS report made policy recommendations to this effect:[13] "Congressional leaders remain worried about implementation of the rebalance, particularly efforts to counter

11 See Stephen Biddle and Ivan Oelrich,"Future Warfare in the Western Pacific: Chinese Antiaccess/Area Denial, U.S. AirSea Battle, and Command of the Commons in East Asia," *International Security* 41:1 (Summer 2016): 2-48..

12 See Stefan Halper, *China: The Three Warfares* (May 2013) for his assumptions specifically related to the South China Sea and the East China Sea. He argues that "China is using the Senkaku Island dispute to probe U.S. intentions, resolve and willingness to defend Japan." (p.10).

13 Michael Green et al., *Asia-Pacific Rebalance 2025 Capabilities, Presence, and Partnerships: An Independent Review of U.S. Defense Strategy in the Asia-Pacific*, CSIS, January 2016.

Chinese coercion in the South China Sea." (p. 195); "U.S. will have to work with its allies and partners to examine deterrence and escalation dynamics in "gray zone' conflicts" (p. 197); and "The U.S. will need to work with Japan, South Korea, Australia, and India to help provide critical platforms enabling systems, training, and maintenance capabilities." (p. 199)

As an extension of their competition to gain wider support from their neighbors, both China and Japan have engaged in regional security and military affairs. They include proving extensive ODAs, donating weapons and military equipment. The recent double-handed summit meetings of the Philippine President Duterte with China's Xi Jinping and Japan's Shinzo Abe are the typical cases in point. His efforts to gain maximum benefits from both of the two great powers may have both positive and negative consequences.

Implications for Regional Security

First and foremost, since the end of WWI, the East China Sea has been one of the choke points in the Asia-Pacific. The occasional incidents in the East China Sea involving maritime clashes between Japan and China over territorial sovereignty, fishing rights, and exploration of oil and gas fields may be just a tip of an iceberg of the huge and fierce competition between the established powers of Japan and the U.S. on the one hand and a rising power of China on the other. Many other countries in the Asia-Pacific have been wooed by and joined these two opposing blocs. Under the leadership of the United States many of its allies and partners have bandwagonned the U.S. pivot and rebalance strategy, while China has been successful in bringing some other countries on its bandwagon and still other countries have developed their own hedging strategy between the two blocs.

Second, the on-going maritime disputes in the South China Sea clearly eclipse the much longer maritime disputes and incident in the East China Sea. China's unprecedented massive construction of artificial islands and military facilities and the debates of the freedom of navigation and airspace have dominated the agendas for many international security forums.

Third, the ideas of oil and gas development projects in the East China Sea have highlighted China's growing oil and gas consumption, a concomitant need to protect its Sea Lines of Communication, and more importantly to defend against the perceived US-led encirclement, if not containment, strategy vis-a-vis China. Due to emerging technologies for alternative energy sources, global energy saving campaigns, and plummeting oil prices, China and Japan have seemingly lost their interest in focusing on the particular aspect of the East China Sea maritime dispute. What is worse, there has been little progress in extracting oil and gas from the contending sea-bed fields.

Fourth, China's stubborn eagerness to break the status quo and to challenge what it perceives as the U.S. strategy of containment in disguise of pivot or rebalance has prompted its A2/AD strategy and the U.S. Air-Sea Battle concept. These developments have led the two big powers to heavily invest in their naval power and also similar measures among their friends and allies in the Western Pacific.

Fifth, there have emerged overlapping and conflicting air Defence identification zones (ADIZs) declared by almost all regional powers including China. These ADIZs may not pose any immediate threats to their neighboring countries, if consulted and handled properly. Political CBMs and military CBMs should be negotiated to prevent the latent collisions and casualties from happening.

Sixth, the combined impact of history, law, psychology and public opinion on the security strategies and military plans of the countries in the East China Sea is invariably huge. Emphasis on the legal aspect of maritime disputes alone can hardly solve the problems,

Seventh and finally, questions abound regarding the prospects for maritime disputes in the East China Sea. For one, China's real intent behind what has been known as the String of Pearl strategy and the One Belt, One Road (OBOR) initiative has been sought after by the U.S. and Japan, who see their security strategies increasingly in conflict particularly with China's maritime Silk Road. Similarly, implications of the so-called Three Warfares by the PLA may need to be explored. Also, according to the "Steps to War" Theory by Paul D. Senese and John A. Vasquez,[14] a military clash would be more likely in the East China Sea than in the South China Sea. Closer coordination is required of on how to avoid these militarized inter-state disputes (MID).

14 Paul D. Senese and John A. Vasquez, *The Steps to War: An Empirical Study* (New Jersey: PrincetonUniversity), 2008.

Geopolitics of the East Sea Disputes and its Implications for Regional Stability

Ngo Thanh Tung

Geo-political importance of the East Sea

The East Sea (or South China Sea) is a semi-closed sea of 3.5 million square meters, which spreads from 3 to 26 degrees North latitude and from 100 to 121 degrees East longitude. The East Sea is surrounded by 9 countries namely Vietnam, China, the Philippines, Indonesia, Brunei, Malaysia, Singapore, Thailand and Cambodia. The East Sea has direct impacts on about 300 million people living in these countries. In addition, it is of great strategic importance to not only regional countries but also to the whole Asia-Pacific.

The East Sea has rich natural resources, which play important roles in people's life and economic development of surrounding countries, especially in terms of fishing, oil exploring and tourism. In the region, China, Thailand, Vietnam, Indonesia and the Philippines are among the world's leading countries in fishing and aquaculture harvests. It is estimated that fish production of regional countries account for around 7 to 8 percent of total fish production all over the world. Meanwhile, the East Sea contains a considerable oil reserve of the world. It is the rich resources in the East Sea that fuel claims over the Paracel Islands and Spratly Islands and surrounding waters.

The East Sea encompasses the world's second busiest international sea line of communication which connects the Pacific with the Indian Ocean, Asia with Europe, and the Middle East with Asia. More than 90 percent of the world's trade volume is carried by sea, of which 45 percent through the East Sea area. There are from 150 to 200 vessels of all kinds traversing daily through the East Sea, of which around 50 percent are vessels of over 5,000 tons and over 10 percent are ones of over 30,000 tons. Maritime trade and industry are increasingly developed in the region. Many East Asian countries relies their economies on this sea line of communication, such as Japan, South Korea, Taiwan, Singapore and even China. The East Sea also contains 29 among 39 shipping lanes of China, whose about 60 percent of import and export volume and 70 percent of imported oil are carried through this area. As for the US, this is the main operational area of its 7th Fleet and transportation route for a large trading volume of itself and its alliances.

Islands and archipelagos in the East Sea are of great strategic importance to many countries' Defence. Paracel and Spratly Islands have strategic positions, which can be used to control sea lines of communication and form bases for military and non-military activities in the East Sea. Strategic analysts believe that if a country could control the Spratly Island, it will be able to control the whole East Sea.

With its essential strategic position, the East Sea is of great importance to regional countries in terms of economy, Defence, security and maritime transportation.

Disputes in the East Sea

As regards to current disputes in the East Sea, the area is a hot spot with territorial disputes among 5 states/ 6 parties (Vietnam, China, the Philippines, Malaysia, Brunei, and Taiwan). The number of incidents, level of tension relating to territorial disputes in the East Sea is on the rise. In 2002, ASEAN and China signed a Declaration of Conducts of the Parties in the South China Sea (DOC) in order to build confidence and control tension escalation in the area. However, since 2009, disputes in the East Sea have been heightened to a new level after China officially declared its "nine-dash-line" claim, which covers over 80 percent of the East Sea area, without any legal basis. In the first half of 2010, China began to consider the East Sea as its "core interest". As a result, since late 2013, China has launched its large-scale construction of artificial islands from its occupied submerged and low-tide elevation features in the East Sea and gradually militarized the islands. As disputes escalated, the East Sea became a common concern of regional and related extra regional countries, as well as a hot topic at almost regional and international multilateral forums. In 2010, at the 17th ASEAN Regional Forum (ARF) Meeting in Hanoi, the US Secretary of State Hillary Clinton stated that freedom of navigation on the East Sea was of the US's national interests. Many other extra-regional countries have also affirmed their interests in freedom of navigation and over flight and gradually engaged in the region. As such, disputes in the East Sea have been of international concerns. Territorial disputes in the East Sea are not only the issue among directly-related parties but also a geo-political concern of many Asia-Pacific countries in terms of peace, stability, security, safety and freedom of navigation and over flight. Strategic competition among major powers, especially the US and China, relating the East Sea, increases, which makes the regional situation more and more complicated.

Implications of East Sea disputes for the region and the world

Firstly, the trend of military and defence build-up, especially naval forces, can erode confidence among countries and create a risk of arms race in the region.

The 21st century is considered as a century of oceans. The rising trend of geo-political factors in East Sea disputes goes with the rising role of sea in development strategies of regional countries. Small coastal countries make all effort to protect their maritime boundaries for their national existence space. Meanwhile, major countries seek to expand their maritime boundaries through disputes to maximize their territorial waters, serving their strategies of maritime power. In order to have advantages in current and future disputes, involved parties and countries focus resources on developing maritime power such as increasing Naval and maritime strength, as well as capacity to control islands in the East Sea. China released a great maritime power strategy, with a focus on building up a strong PLAN. In May 2015, China released its Defence White Paper, which stated that PLAN would combine "offshore waters Defence" and "open sea protection", instead of just focusing on "offshore waters Defence", to deal with any threat to China's sovereignty. South East Asian countries such as the Philippines, Indonesia and Vietnam are also increasing their Navy and Coast Guard capacities on different scales. The increasing expenditure on Defence stems from these countries' needs for defence modernization in order to increase their Defence capacity, protect their interests and sovereignty, catch up with the current military revolution, and meet the expanded roles of the military (dealing with non-traditional security challenges and international cooperation). Besides, the unsolved sovereignty disputes in South China Sea and the lack of trust and confidence between countries also contribute to the increase in Defence investment and expenditure. An arms race is looming in the region. These issues, if not well managed and controlled, are likely to lead to armed conflicts.

Secondly, accelerating island militarization, increasing military presence and activities on the East Sea will raise risks of military collisions, tensions and conflicts.

The maritime features play an important military role. They can be considered as "offshore military outpost". Because of their strategic advantages, recently China has conducted large-scale construction of artificial islands on some of its occupied features in the Spratly in combination with acceleration of militarization on these newly-built islands, including the installation of a HQ-9 SAM system on Woody Island in the Paracel, building runways and airports on islands in the Spratlys (Fiery Cross Reef; Mischief Reef; and Subi Reef). A Chinese military aircraft landed at the Fiery Cross Reef for the first time on 17 April 2016. Besides, China has increased military exercises in the East Sea. In May 2016, PLA held a large-scale exercise "with the aim to enhance combat readiness and coordination between ships, aircrafts and forces". From 19 to 21July 2016, South Sea Fleet of PLAN launched the exercise in the Paracels. From 11 19 September 2016, Russia joined the "Joint Sea 2016" exercise with China in the East Sea. At the same time, China indicated its intention and readiness to establish ADIZ in the East Sea. Other countries have raised their concerns about China's enhanced control of the East Sea.

The US continues to maintain and enhance the military presence in the East Sea for ensuring the international waters for all countries. In Mar 2016, the aircraft carrier USS John C. Stennis, with the escort of the cruiser USS Mobile Bay, destroyers USS Stockdale and USS Chung-Hoon, had a routine patrol in the East Sea. In June 2016, two aircraft carriers USS John C. Stennis and USS Ronald Reagan took part in the exercises for the first time in the East Sea. On 17 August 2016, a flight wing of B-52, B-1 Lancer and B-2 Spirit had the first patrol flight over the East Sea. According to Admiral Richardson, the large-scale island reclamation and militarization by China in the East Sea create potential threats for freedom of navigation in the region and the US is forced to react. Besides, the US is currently increasing their military support and presence in the Philippines.

Japan also states that it will increase its engagement in the East Sea. On 15 September 2016, Japanese Defence Minister, Tomomi Inada spoke at CSIS, pointing out that "Japan strongly supports the US Navy's Freedom of Navigation Operations, which go a long way to upholding the rules-based international maritime order. Japan on its part will increase its engagement in the East Sea through, for example, Maritime Self-Defence Force joint training cruises with the US Navy, bilateral and multi-lateral exercises with coastal navies".

On 5 June 2016, speaking at Shangri-La Dialogue in Singapore, French Defence Minister Jean-Yves Le Drian urged navies of European countries to have a permanent and effective presence in the East Sea. "If we want to control the risk of conflict, we have to protect ourselves. Since the start of this year, our navy has already been deployed three times to the East Sea".

There is a likelihood that, the East Sea will become an area of high military sensitivity with the increase of military activities of countries in this region. On 17 May 2016, the US DoD announced two Chinese fighter aircraft unsafely intercepted US surveillance aircraft EP-3 in the East Sea international airspace. It can be seen that a clear tendency of military activities is increasing in the East Sea. These are potential threats to regional security and stability in the near future. If this issue is not properly managed, risks will increase, leading to instability, conflicts, and negative effects on rights and interests of many regional and extra-regional countries in terms of strategies, politics, security, economics, and trade, etc.

Thirdly, major powers utilize the East Sea issue as reason to gather forces to restrain and compete with each other, forcing small countries to take sides in this competition. This can lead to the risk of confrontation, a new type of Cold War in the region.

The US "rebalance" strategy to the Asia-Pacific has been launched with the aim to comprehensively engage in the region, in which the US consolidates political, military and security ties with its regional alliances, as well as extends its partnerships. The US also increases presence in the East Sea through activities of periodic patrols and encourages regional countries join these activities. It also warns and prevents China's construction and militarization of islands in the East Sea. Partners and allies of the US in the region consider its presence as insurance for regional security and stability amid the rise of China.

Meanwhile, China proposes regional and trans-regional initiatives, fosters multi-faceted cooperation with ASEAN, utilizes its soft and economic power to seduce regional and ASEAN members both bilaterally and multilaterally. China makes use of the economic interdependence in the region to seduce other countries to support its position on the East Sea issues, and be ready to respond to US activities in this area.

The increasing competition between China and US in the Asia-Pacific as well as their conflicting interests in the East Sea is complicating the situation and is strongly affecting other smaller countries and ASEAN members. The failure of the ASEAN Ministerial Meeting 45 (AMM 45) in 2012 and the 3rd ASEAN Defence Ministers' Meeting (ADMM+) in 2015 in releasing their Joint Statements pointed out the fact that ASEAN was severely affected by the competition of outer major powers. ASEAN also showed its incapability of managing its relations with these two major powers. These issues have posed challenges to the central and leading roles of ASEAN as well as the solidarity and consensus of this organization not only in dealing with the East Sea disputes but also in other regional related issues.

Fourthly, fostering national interests, increasing activities claiming sovereignty without abiding to laws could undermine international order and laws as well as have impacts on many countries, especially small regional ones.

Unilateral activities have made the East Sea become a concern of not only disputed countries but also international and regional community by increasing tension and threatening to freedom of navigation and over flight, regional peace and stability as well as exercising of international law. These activities can be listed as expanding disputed areas, increasing field activities such as conducting large-scale reclamation, issuing fishing bans, militarizing occupied islands, and harassing other countries' fishermen. On 5 June 2016, giving speech at the Shangri-La Dialogue at Singapore, the French Defence Minister, Jean - Yves Le Drian stated that the East Sea disputes were also of concern to the EU and the world. He also said that unless the Law of Sea was strictly abided to in this region, it could be challenged in the Mediterranean Sea or the Arctic Ocean. In one of recent speech made in a Nikkei-organized conference, Singaporean President Lee Hsien Loong emphasized that the East Sea disputes needed to be addressed through international laws, if "law of the jungle" prevailed, small countries would be controlled by bigger and more powerful ones.

On 12 July 2016, the Permanent Court of Arbitration released its verdict on the legal case of the Philippines against China about the East Sea. The Court provided a new set of regulations about all features at sea. This is a legal turning point in the East Sea disputes as well as a basis for the international community to assess these disputes based on international laws. The verdict about historical right of the "nine-dash line", and the conclusion that features in the Spratlys are rocks, not islands (in their nature conditions) indirectly narrowed down the disputed areas among related countries. Although China rejected the rulings of the PCA and the verdict has not changed the status quo of the disputes in short term, experts believe that this is the final conclusion, which has legal values and capability to open a new page for disputes in the East Sea.

Conclusion

The East Sea is of great strategic and geo-political importance to countries in the Asia-Pacific. Recently, disputes in the East Sea has had complex developments such as expanding disputed zones, conducting unilateral field activities to claim sovereignty without abiding to international law and causing regional tensions. Sovereignty disputes on the East Sea are not limited to related countries only but they have also became international issues because of its direct implications to regional peace, stability as well as security, safety, freedom of navigation and over flight and strategic interests of many regional and extra-regional countries. In order to safeguard a peaceful and stable environment, all countries are to exercise self-restraint, avoid escalating tensions and settle disputes on the basis of international law. Regional countries also need to construct codes of conduct at sea in addressing disputes, foster confidence building and cooperation for regional peace and stability. ASEAN and China are to achieve Codes of Conduct for Parties on the East Sea issue "(COC) at an early date.

References

1. TranBong, “Bien Dong: Dia chien luoc va tiemnangkinh te”, Nghiencuu bien Dong, Feb 29, 2009, http://nghiencuubiendong.vn/tong-quan-ve-bien-dong/504-bien-ong-ia-chien-lc-va-tiem-nng (accessedOctober 11, 2016)

2. Ha Anh Tuan, «Yeu to chien luoctrongthamvong Bien Dong cua Trung Quoc», Nghiencuu bien Dong, June 17, 2016, http://nghiencuubiendong.vn/nghien-cuu-vietnam/5937-yeu-to-chien-luoc-trong-tham-vong-bien-dong-cua-trung-quoc (accessedOctober 11, 2016)

3. Nguyen Ngoc Truong, “Ve van de Bien Dong”, Nhaxuat ban Chinh tri quocgia, March-2014, http://www.nxbctqg.org.vn/index.php?option=com_content&view=article&id=4158:v-vn-bin-ong&catid=169:bin-o-que-hng&Itemid=641 (accessed October 11, 2016)

4. Remarks by Jean-Yves Le Drian, Minister of Defence, France at the 15th Shangri-la Dialogue, Singapore, 03-05 June, 2016.

5. “Chinese military aircraft makes first public landing on disputed island”, Reuters, Industrials, Apr 17, 2016, http://www.reuters.com/article/southchinasea-china-idUSL3N17L1M8 (accessed October 11, 2016).

6. Franz-Stefan Gady for The Diplomat, “China's Navy Conducts South China Sea Drills Involving Paracel and Spratly Islands”, The Diplomat, May 05, 2016, http://thediplomat.com/2016/05/chinas-navy-conducts-south-china-sea-drills-involving-paracel-and-spratly-islands/ (accessed October 11, 2016).

7. David Larter, “The U.S. just sent a carrier strike group to confront China”, Navytimes,March 3, 2016, https://www.navytimes.com/story/military/2016/03/03/stennis-strike-group-deployed-to-south-china-sea/81270736/ (accessed October 12, 2016).

8. Megan Eckstein,“Stennis, Reagan CSGs Conduct Dual-Carrier Operations In Philippine Sea”, USNI News, June 20, 2016, https://news.usni.org/2016/06/20/stennis-reagan-dual-carrier-operations (accessed October 13, 2016).

9. David Cenciotti, “B-52, B-1 and B-2 simultaneously conduct missions from Guam in unprecedented integrated bomber operation in Pacific”, The Aviationist, Aug 17 2016, https://theaviationist.com/2016/08/17/b-52-b-1-and-b-2-simultaneously-conduct-missions-from-guam-in-unprecedented-integrated-bomber-operation-in-pacific/ (accessed October 11, 2016).

10. "US: 2 aircaft carriers to deter China", Philippine daily Inquirer, June 22, 2016, http://www.pressreader.com/ (accessed October 10, 2016).

11. Tomomi Inada's speech at CSIS, "Evolving the Japan – US Alliance-- Keeping Asia Pacific peaceful and Prosperous", September 15, 2016, https://csis-prod.s3.amazonaws.com/s3fs-public/event/160915_Tomomi_Inada_transcript.pdf (accessed October 12, 2016).

12. "Chinese fighter jets intercept US spy plane 'unsafely' over South China Sea", AFP, May 18, 2016.

13. Kentaro Iwamoto, "Singapore PM warns against 'law of the jungle' in South China Sea", Asia Review, September 29, 2016, http://asia.nikkei.com/Politics-Economy/International-Relations/Singapore-PM-warns-against-law-of-the-jungle-in-South-China-Sea (accessed October 9,2016).

China's Perspective on the Maritime Disputes in the Western Pacific

Mu Changlin

First, I want to thank the USI of India for inviting me to attend this seminar. I would like to take this opportunity to share with you some of my personal understanding of China's perspective on maritime disputes in the Western Pacific.

China is a coastal state with a coastline of over 18,000 kilometers, adjacent or opposite to eight neighboring countries, surrounding the Yellow Sea, the East China Sea and the South China Sea. The eight countries are Democratic People's republic of Korea (DPRK), Republic of Korea (ROK), Japan, Vietnam, the Philippines, Malaysia, Brunei and Indonesia. As you know, China and Japan have disputes on the sovereignty over the Diaoyu Islands. China, Vietnam, the Philippines, and Malaysia have disputes on the sovereignty over the Nansha Islands. Along with the establishment of the new international order of the seas and oceans through the 1982 UNCLOS, the overlapping claims over the EEZ and the continental shelf between China and these eight countries emerged. In the Yellow Sea, China needs to divide the border of territorial waters, EEZ and continental shelf with North Korea; divide the border of EEZ and continental shelf with South Korea.

Let me take the South China Sea issue as an example. China was the first to discover, to name, to exercise administrative jurisdiction and to develop the islands and reefs in the South China Sea. China's sovereignty over Nasnha Islands was never questioned until 1970s, when large amounts of oil and gas resources were discovered in the South China Sea and the EEZ system was negotiated, and some countries illegally occupied

42 islands and reefs of China's Nansha Islands. After the signing of the UNCLOS in 1982, some countries gradually put forward their claims over the EEZ, the continental shelf and other maritime rights, and some of these claims overlapped. These factors make the South China Sea issue more complicated.

Recently, the South China Sea issue has caught the attention of the world and one of the major reasons is that the arbitration tribunal of the South China Sea made a ruling in July, 2016. So why has China taken the position of non-participation and non-acceptance of the arbitration?

In fact, China and the Philippines have acknowledged many times in their early documents regarding their bilateral relations that they would resolve their disputes over the South China Sea through negotiations. In addition, both China and the Philippines have signed the DOC, which stipulates clearly to resolve their territorial and jurisdictional disputes by peaceful means. That the Philippines filed a case to a third party for arbitration on its disputes with China over the South China Sea has violated these commitments and the principle of "agreements must be kept" ("pactasuntservanda").

The case filed by the Philippines relates to the sovereignty disputes over some of the islands and reefs of the Nansha Islands, which is an integral part of the maritime delimitation between China and the Philippines. The UNCLOS has no right to mediate the dispute, as it is a territorial issue. In 2006, China made an exclusive statement on the basis of Article 298 of the UNCLOS to exclude disputes over maritime delimitation from the Convention's dispute settlement mechanism. More than 30 countries including China have made such exclusive statements, which formed a part of the UNCLOS's dispute settlement mechanism. So China's position is fully in accordance with the international law including the UNCLOS.

In such a complicated situation, China has always exercised a high-level of self-restraint and approached the disputes in a constructive and responsible manner. China's position and policies in dealing with the maritime disputes are given below:

The first is to maintain peace and stability in the South China Sea. As the biggest coastal state of the South China Sea, China has always been committed to the realization of its peaceful development and would never like to see turmoil and wars taking place in its surrounding regions, maintaining peace and stability of the South China Sea is in line with China's best interests. With joint efforts of China and its neighboring countries, the South China Sea situation remained relatively stable for a long time. Currently, the South China Sea is one of the busiest maritime passages in the world that offers the safest navigation. From the 1990s to 2015, the total trade volume between China and the ASEAN countries has jumped 60 times from less than US$ 8 billion to US$ 472.2 billion, and the economic aggregate of most of the ASEAN countries has grown more than 5 times respectively. As practice has proved, it is not fearsome that disputes exist in maritime rights between nations, as long as the countries concerned take the spirits of sincerity, mutual understanding and insist on resolution of the disputes by peaceful means.

The second is to resolve maritime disputes peacefully through consultations and negotiations. While firmly safeguarding the territorial sovereignty and maritime rights, China has never stopped making efforts to negotiate with countries directly concerned to resolve their disputes on the basis of historical facts and international laws. In the past 50 years, China has signed boundary treaties with 12 of its 14 neighbors on land. These treaties involved over 20,000 kilometers of boundary, accounting for 90 percent of China's land borders. These are examples of how China has resolved disputes through face-to-face negotiations with other countries directly involved in the disputes. In 2014, China and some ASEAN countries proposed the dual-track concept for resolving the South China Sea issue, namely the disputes should be resolved peacefully by countries directly concerned through consultations and negotiations, peace and stability of the South China Sea should be maintained jointly by China and the ASEAN countries. China has also engaged in bilateral negotiation and cooperation with claimers concerned. China and Vietnam, through consultation on the equal basis, have defined their respective territorial waters, EEZ and continental shelf in the Beibu Gulf. The China-Vietnam steering committee on the bilateral relations meets annually to discuss how to deal with their maritime disputes properly and promote maritime cooperation. China and Vietnam have started joint exploration outside the outlet of the Beibu Gulf and set up working groups to discuss how to engage in joint development of the Beibu Gulf and the South China Sea to a larger extent. China and the Philippines have once achieved consensus on maintaining self-restraint in the South China Sea and not taking actions that would aggravate the situation through several consultations of the China-Philippine working group on confident building measures in the South China Sea. China has also maintained close communication with Malaysia, Indonesia and Brunei to properly manage and control the situation of the South China Sea and promote maritime cooperation. During Philippine President Duterte's visit to China last month, China and the Philippines agreed to address the South China Sea disputes "through friendly consultations and negotiations by sovereign states directly concerned". Experiences have shown that consultations and negotiations are the most realistic and effective approach to resolve the maritime disputes.

The third is to control differences through making rules and establishing mechanisms. China believes that before the resolution of the disputes, all parties concerned would manage and control the disputes by rules or mechanisms to ensure regional peace and stability. In 2002, China and ASEAN countries signed the DOC. So far, 13 Senior Officials' Meetings and 18 joint working group meetings have been held. In September 2013, China and ASEAN countries officially launched the negotiation of the COC, which has made significant progress in 3 years, formed two consensus documents and two open documents. Negotiations are now entering a new phase of "important and complex issues". At the 13th Senior Officials' Meeting held in China this year, China and ASEAN agreed that they will try to conclude a draft framework of the COC by the mid of next year, under the condition of no outside interference. China and ASEAN have already achieved "Early Harvest Measures", including the "Hotline Platform on Search and Rescue among China and ASEAN Member States", the "Senior Officials' Hotline Platform in Response to Maritime Emergencies among Ministries of Foreign Affairs of China and ASEAN Member States". China and ASEAN have also agreed to establish "Preventive Measures to Manage Risks at Sea", which will serve as the interim measures prior to the final conclusion of the COC.

The fourth is to maintain the freedom of navigation and over-flight. Every year, there are about one hundred thousand ships passing freely and safely through the South China Sea, which carry more than 70 percent of the world's international trade, none of them has ever run into any problem with freedom of navigation. The annual import and export commodities trade of China amounts to US$4.3 trillion, about 85 percent of which passing through the South China Sea. This means that China cares more than any other country about freedom of navigation and over-flight in the South China Sea. Some people worried that China's construction on the islands and reefs will hinder the freedom of navigation and over-flight and led to "militarization" of the South China Sea. In fact, in addition to necessary Defence facilities, China's construction on the islands and reefs of the South China Sea is mainly for civilian purposes, it is to provide public products to the international community. I want to point out that China is not the first country to deploy weapons in Nansha Islands, is not the country with the largest deployment of weapon, nor it is the country conducted the most frequent military activities.

The fifth is to achieve win-win cooperation. China values friendly and cooperative relationship with its neighbors. China has taken the initiative to call on all parties involved to "shelve differences and engage in joint development" in the South China Sea. This provides a useful approach to the resolution of the issue. This is an approach that takes into consideration of the interests of all parties concerned. In 2005, oil companies from China, Vietnam and the Philippines signed the "Agreement for Joint Marine Seismic Undertaking in Certain Areas in the South China Sea". This was an effort for joint development of oil and gas resources in the South China Sea. In 2011, China announced the establishment of China-ASEAN Maritime Cooperation Fund with a total of 3 billion RMB Yuan. Up to now, more than 40 maritime cooperation projects have been launched. Two years ago, China put forward the initiative of the 21st century Maritime Silk Road. These measures and initiatives are evidence of China's efforts and good faith in seeking further and deeper cooperation with its neighbors.

In conclusion, I believe that China and the countries concerned have the wisdom and ability to resolve their maritime disputes through consultations and negotiations and jointly maintain the peace and stability in the Western Pacific.

Dynamics of Indo-Pak and Sino-Indo Border Dispute and its Implications on Stability of South Asia

Maj Gen RPS Badauria, VSM (Retd)

In a globalized world of interconnected societies and transnational threats, where borders seem to be more a geographical expression rather than demarcation of national interests, territorial disputes remind us that sovereignty still matters. Today, there are seventy-one unresolved territorial disputes involving over 40 per cent of sovereign states. Of all interstate disputes, ones over territory tend to be nearly twice as likely as other issues to lead to armed conflict. Drawing boundaries between countries has always been a very politically sensitive, especially when governments or groups of people have a particular stake in a geographic area.

The troubles in South Asia, its endemic tensions, mutual distrust and occasional hostilities are largely considered products of the contradictions of India's security perception with that of the rest of the countries. Whereas India considers neighbours as an integral part of its own security system, the neighbours feel threatened by some of India's actions. The pre-eminence of India in the South Asian power configuration given its geography, demography, economics, and ecology is something about which neither India nor its neighbours can do nothing but accept that India is central to politico-economic- security architecture of the sub-continent. India has embarked on 'Neighbourhood First" policy which has resulted in improved relations with all its neighbours except Pakistan. South Asia is one of the least inter- connected region yet it will be the fastest growing region and India will be central to this growth in the coming years.

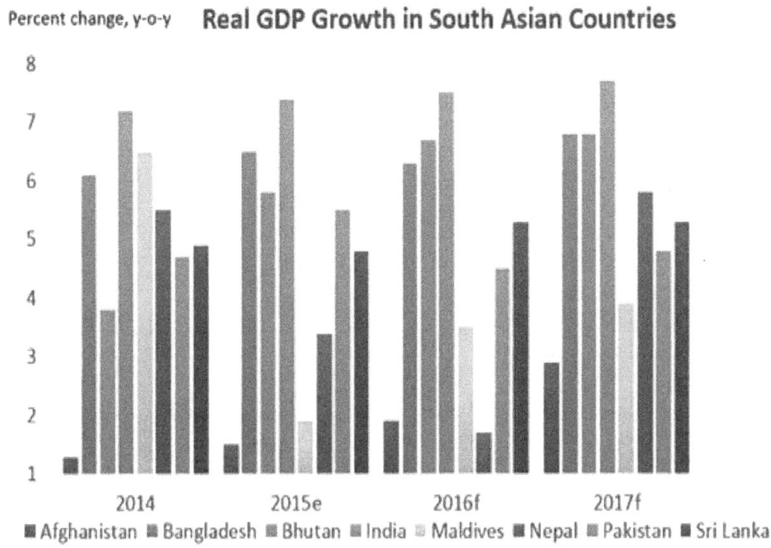

Indo-Pak Border Dispute

The perceptions about the dispute vary on both sides of the border. India's position is that the Indian Independence Act of 1947 did not allocate Kashmir to Pakistan; rather allowed the princely state to select the dominion of its choice. And that Pakistan started the first war of Kashmir by dispatching militants who enjoyed various levels of state support in an effort to seize Kashmir by force, despite having signed a standstill agreement which bound it to not undertake a military invasion. As a consequence of Pakistan's invasion in 1947, the Maharaja of Kashmir Hari Singh signed an instrument of accession to India in exchange for military assistance. Thus, all of Kashmir, including that portion currently administered by Pakistan and that portion "ceded" to China in 1963, are lawful parts of India.

As regards to physical control of the territory of Jammu & Kashmir (J&K), out of 2,22,236 sq km, the PoK has 78,114 sq km i.e. 35.15 percent; China occupies 42,735 sq km i.e. 19.23 percent of the total area that also includes the territory (5,180 sq km) of Shaksgam–Murtagh Valley ceded to China by Pakistan through Sino Pakistan Frontier Agreement of March 02, 1963. Inside PoK, the so called 'Azad Kashmir' (Mirpur, Poonch) has 13,297 sq km of territory with it and the rest is known as Northern Areas of Gilgit and Baltistan.

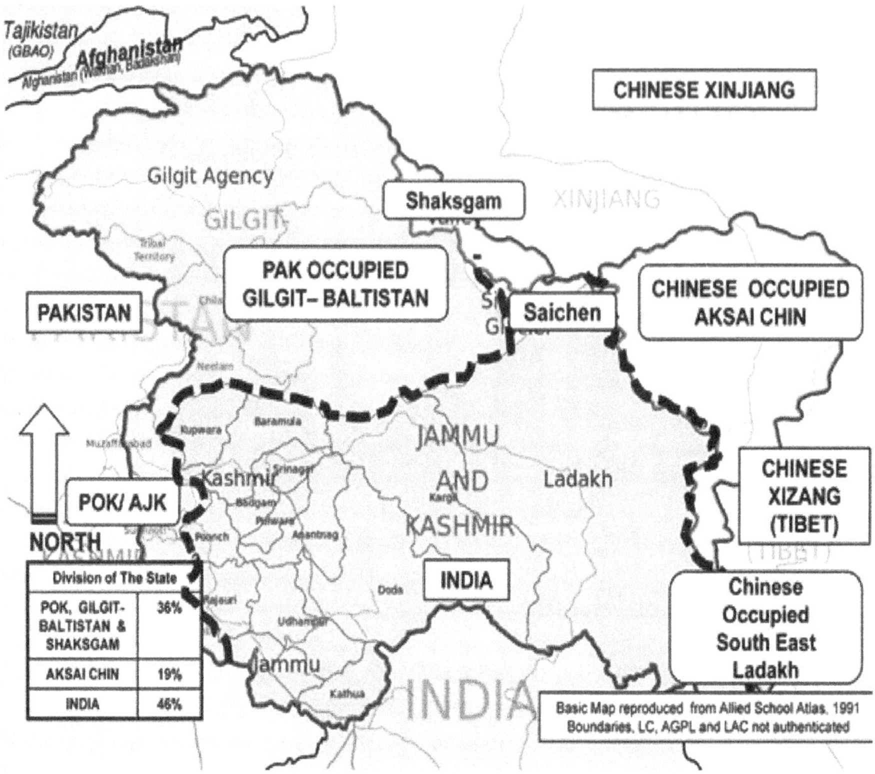

Pakistan- a Revisionist State Baroness Nicholson, European Parliament Rapporteur for Kashmir had said in a report that on the basis of all the maps, treaties including the lease agreement of 1935, historic documents and speeches, putting together a comprehensive picture from 1846 until 2007, it is proven that Gilgit and Baltistan were in the domain of the Maharaja of Jammu and Kashmir. It also formed part of the instrument of accession, signed by Maharaja Hari Singh on October 26, 1947. She has elaborated further "all the evidence points to the fact that Gilgit and Baltistan regions were constituents of Jammu and Kashmir by 1877, under the sovereignty of Maharaja Gulab Singh, and remained in the domain of the independent princely state, up to and including the formation of India and Pakistan on August 15, 1947." After the signing of the Instrument of Accession, the J&K Constituent assembly also later ratified the Instrument of Accession, thereby, completing all the legal formalities pertaining to a lawful merger of J&K in India.

Pakistan's lack of sovereignty on PoK is illustrated by Asif Ezdi, a former member of the Pakistan Foreign Service who in 2009 had in an article written that "The Pakistan Constitution is completely silent on the Kashmir status. Article 257, which is a reproduction of identical provisions in the 1956 and 1962 constitutions, deals only with the future status of the state and reads as follows: When the people of the State of Jammu and Kashmir decide to accede to Pakistan, the relationship between Pakistan and that state shall be determined in accordance with the wishes of the people of that state".

On the other hand, the Constitution of India has kept a provision of additional five seats in the Lok Sabha, over and above 545, that can be filled up from PoK once the area is freed. The Indian side of J&K Assembly has 24 seats earmarked for the areas under PoK, nonetheless, not filled as the territory is under foreign occupation. The Indian sovereignty on entire J&K is legally unassailable.

Thus it is amply clear that India is the status-quo power on Kashmir and Pakistan is the revisionist state seeking territorial changes through the use of military force (1947-48, 1965, 1999) and through terrorist proxies (1947-present). Not only does Pakistan lack any defensible equities in Kashmir, India has been the victim of Pakistan's reliance upon Islamist militant proxies in Kashmir literally since 1947. Therefore, one needs to consider following issues:-

- Is the problem between India & Pakistan only about territorial dispute?
- Will resolution of Kashmir dispute bring peace and stability in South Asia ?

Formation of Pakistan On the Basis of Two Nation Theory. In its simplest way it means the cultural, political, religious, economic and social dissimilarities between the two major communities, Hindus and Muslims of the Sub Continent. These differences of outlook, in fact, were instrumental in giving rise to two distinct political ideologies. Pakistan believes that the story of Pakistan began not during the Pakistan Movement, but with the invasion of Sindh by Arab commander, Muhammad bin Qasim, in the 9th Century who defeated the region's Hindu ruler, Raja Dahir; this is the basis for the formation of Pakistan.

Pakistani journalist Babar Ayaz in his book on 'What's Wrong With Pakistan?' says Muslims in India, after 650 years of rule in which they never thought of themselves as a separate nation, suddenly work up around 1857 to the fact that they may be a relative minority in a democratic polity of the future. Ayaz, quoting Stephen Cohen of Brookings, says: "Iqbal's idea of Pakistan was not based on a European model of a nation-state, but on 'an acute understanding that political power was essential to the higher end of establishing God's laws.'"

India's position is that it is a secular country and people of all faith and religion are part of it with equal rights and that there can be no discrimination on the basis of the religion. Therefore, merger of a Muslim dominated state with India debunks the basic premise on which Pakistan was created.

Pakistan - an Ideological State. The first constitution of Pakistan defined it as an Islamic state and the bastion of Islam. Soon after partition, Muslim League used Islam, though unsuccessfully, to dissolve the ethnic nationalism and integrate the newly formed nation. Later President Zia remarked that Pakistan was conceived as theocratic entity and introduced many features of Sharia laws, he brought all the elements of Iqbal's flawed genetic idea together by making jihad central to the Pakistani army and the state it owns. He believed that the Army must protect this ideology and the strategy that he adopted was use of Jihad and it continues even till date. Every army chief says the two-nation theory is their ideology and the army protects their ideology and geography. Pakistani citizens are made to believe that their nationhood is under constant threat from India and it represents an existential threat to Pakistan – source of military's dominance in affairs of country. The traditional focus of the Pakistan armed forces has been on combating a perceived threat from India and as part of its strategy to bleed India through thousand cuts, Pakistani intelligence agencies have provided patronage to Islamic extremists in Kashmir in the name of Jihad. Pakistani support for terrorists in Kashmir contributes significantly to tension with India and heightens Indian suspicion that Islamabad is responsible for perpetrating violence within India proper.

Christine Fair puts it bluntly: "Pakistan is an ideological state. The Kashmir issue is not causal, it's symptomatic. Fair found that jihad is central to the Pakistani army's strategic culture: "The use of jihad is a way to make it seem as if everything the Pakistani army does is Islamically justified." If jihad is the army's policy, it is the policy of the Pakistani state too. Moreover, she is of the opinion that feudals in Pakistan can retain their landed riches only by backing the army and its monopoly on power.

Pakistan's Behaviour as a Nuclear Power State. Pakistan's nuclear capabilities are India centric and therefore it follows First Use policy. It is also developing Tactical Nuclear Weapons and is striving for "full spectrum" deterrence under which nuclear weapons will not be used to deter just a nuclear war, but also other threats such as Indian conventional attacks. Reports also suggest that Pakistan could have the third-biggest nuclear stockpile within a decade and could end up producing 20 nuclear warheads annually. Pakistan is a territorially dissatisfied state and is also conventionally weaker power in comparison to India. Moreover, it employs destabilising tactics against India by use of state sponsored terrorism under nuclear umbrella. Pakistani Army has for decades nurtured extremist groups as strategic assets against India and Afghanistan. This has been the main source of security concern in south Asia and India in particular.

Indo – China Border Dispute

Sardar Vallabhbhai Patel in his letter to Jawaharlal Nehru on 7 November 1950 wrote that "Throughout history we have seldom been worried about our north-east frontier. The Himalayas have been regarded as an impenetrable barrier against any threat from the north. We had a friendly Tibet which gave us no trouble". As a consequence to PLA moving in to Tibet in 1950, he wrote "While our western and north-western threat to security is still as prominent as before, a new threat has developed from the north and north-east. Thus, for the first time, after centuries, India's defence has to concentrate itself on two fronts simultaneously". Tibet has not only acted as buffer but also is the source of origin of all the major rivers in Asia. Much later China attacked India in 1962 and annexed large part of its territory in Ladakh.

Though the border dispute remains far from permanent settlement, in the words of S M Krishna, Former Foreign Minister of India in Sep 2009 "As compared to other countries, the Indo-China border is most peaceful ,whenever there are incursions on either side, there is a built-in mechanism which takes care of things." What worries India more than the unresolved border is the growing economic and political differential with China, this is further accentuated by growing China – Pakistan nexus.

Pakistan - China Nexus

China's primary strategic goal in contemporary times has been the accumulation of "comprehensive national power." This pursuit of power in its entire dimensions-economic, military, technological, and diplomatic is driven by the conviction that China, a great civilization undone by the hostility of others, could never attain its destiny unless it amassed the power necessary to ward off the hostility of those opposed to this quest. China wants to be the dominant power in Asia and aspires to be to leading world power. Pakistan on the other hand is still struggling to become a nation state and is facing myriad problems, many of them of its own making. It has realised that it can exploit its geo-strategic location to its advantage and become the ultimate security rentier state. China-Pakistan strategic nexus, therefore, advances the national interests of both the countries.

Pakistan wants to have parity with India; China wants to be the dominant power in the region. Pakistan wants to limit India's regional as well as global role by blocking us westwards so that we don't have easy access to Afghanistan and Central Asia; China wants to confine us to South Asia, keep us entangled in the sub-continent so that we are unable to fully exert our influence in the rest of Asia and beyond, giving China space and time to entrench its influence there without having to face competition from India. Pakistan is determined to confront India and China is intent on giving Pakistan the means and the confidence to continue this confrontation.

It is a reality that India faces two front threat scenario, Pakistan – China strategic nexus is and will remain the most formidable challenge to India's national security. India's Defence capabilities should be geared to deter and defeat collusive hybrid threats from adversaries while maintaining a stable internal security environment. This will also provide stability to the entire region.

The Islamic State's Influence in the Indo-Pacific Region

Sumitha Narayanan Kutty

Introduction

The Islamic State (or the Islamic State of Iraq and the Levant/Syria - ISIL/ ISIS – or its Arabic acronym *Da'esh*), henceforth IS, is today a transnational terrorist group and a quasi-state with formalized governance structures that controls significant areas of Iraq and Syria and, in parallel, fifteen-odd provinces (*wilayat*) around the world. [1] The group has a worldwide following with volunteers and foreign fighters pledging allegiance for reasons that range from the group's specific brand of brutality to the renunciation of modern comforts to lead, what followers believe, is the "true Islamic way of life." [2]

As Iraqi forces launch operations to retake IS strongholds, there is palpable concern among governments around the world regarding fighters who may choose to return to their countries of origin or head to a new safe

1 Figure based on *wilayahs* listed in IS' *Dabiq* magazine (latest version released in July 2016) where its members are currently undertaking operations. *Dabiq: Break the Cross*, Issue 15, 1437 Shawwal, p.40, http://www.clarionproject.org/factsheets-files/islamic-state-magazine-dabiq-fifteen-breaking-the-cross.pdf, accessed on October 15, 2016.

2 Shaju Philip, "How Kerala's missing young men turned hardliners," *The Indian Express*, July 12, 2016, http://indianexpress.com/article/india/india-news-india/kerala-missing-youth-join-islamic-state-isis-2908160/, accessed on August 30, 2016.

haven. [3] It is within this context that the paper examines the influence of the IS in India and, further east, in Southeast Asia.

This paper argues that the threat is essentially local and the networks enabling IS-inspired attacks are largely familiar to security forces in these regions. It does so by first assessing the appeal and impact of the IS through its propaganda and operations in India and key Southeast Asian states such as the Philippines and Indonesia. It will then briefly examine the domestic terror outfits that have pledged allegiance to the IS, like the *Indian Mujahideen*'s splinter group *Ansar-ut Tawhid fi Bilad al-Hind* in India and the *Abu Sayyaf* in the Philippines, following which it highlights a few key state responses to the IS threat. The paper concludes by noting key takeaways that influence our response to this threat going forward.

The Islamic State's Appeal in India and Southeast Asia

It is difficult to make an accurate assessment of fighters from both India and Southeast Asia that have traveled to the IS in Iraq and Syria. According to data compiled by The Soufan Group in 2015, Indonesia made the highest contribution from Southeast Asia last year with around 700 fighters followed by a hundred each from the Philippines and Malaysia while Singapore and Cambodia's contributions remain within single digits. India also ranks low with 23 fighters in Iraq and Syria (unofficially around 50). [4]

---

3 "M'sia warns South-east Asia to be on alert as offensive begins in IS-controlled Mosul," *Today*, October 17, 2016, http://www.todayonline.com/world/asia/msia-warns-south-east-asia-be-alert-offensive-begins-controlled-mosul, accessed on October 20, 2016.

4 "Foreign Fighters: An Updated Assessment of the Flow of Foreign Fighters into Syria and Iraq," The Soufan Group, December 2015, http://soufangroup.com/wp-content/uploads/2015/12/TSG_ForeignFightersUpdate3.pdf, accessed on September 22, 2016.

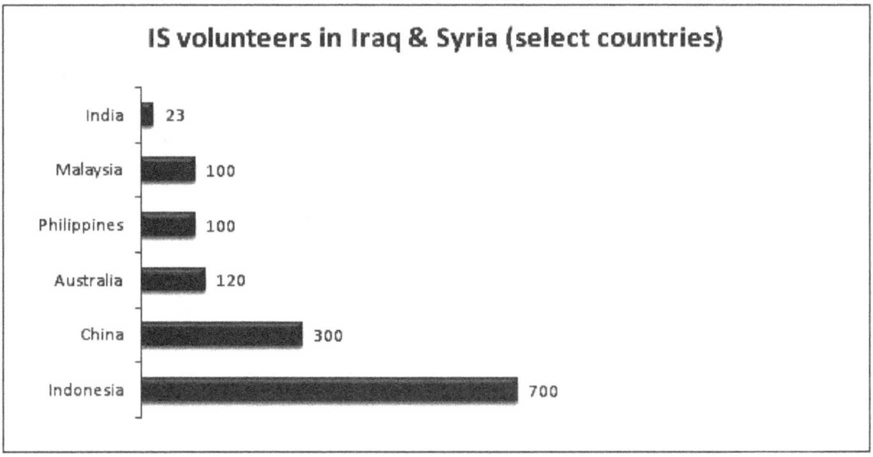

Figure 1. No. of foreign fighters who joined ISIS in Iraq and Syria from select countries. (*Data: The Soufan Group, December 2015)*

Attacks

India is yet to be successfully targeted by IS-inspired operatives, though a number of plots have been foiled in their planning stages. Within Southeast Asia, Indonesia was the first country to be targeted by an IS-inspired attack in January 2016 that killed four civilians. Malaysia witnessed its first IS-labeled attack in June this year when two men threw a grenade into a nightclub in the western state of Selangor wounding eight people. But it is the Philippines that has been designated the "weakest link" in Southeast Asia given the local terror group Abu Sayyaf's hold over the country's southern provinces and its allegiance to the IS. [5] Most recently in September, an explosion in a busy night market killed twelve people in the city of Davao, hometown of Philippine President Rodrigo Duterte.

In spite of the group's global propaganda and public relations exercise, these IS-inspired elements in India and Southeast Asia are principally homegrown. Their networks and assets are largely known quantities to intelligence and security forces and the key to weakening these 'feeder groups', or even defeating them, perhaps lies in this.

5 Joseph Chinyong Liow, "Escalating ISIS threat in Southeast Asia: Is the Philippines a weak link?," *CNN*, July 9, 2016. http://edition.cnn.com/2016/07/07/opinions/isis-southeast-asia-liow/, accessed on September 20, 2016.

IS in India: Underestimation or exaggeration?

The Numbers

From the estimated twenty-three Indians that have joined the Islamic State, six have died in Syria and two are believed to have returned. [6] The group's appeal was first made public in India with the arrest of 23-year-old Arif Majeed in November 2014. [7] The first IS module was busted in May 2015. [8] Between then and August 2016, the National Investigative Agency (NIA), the central agency established to combat terror after the 2008 Mumbai attacks, and various state police have arrested at least 54 individuals and the NIA has charge sheeted 29 of them. [9] A number of individuals have also been reported missing from Kerala, Telangana, Karnataka, Tamil Nadu, Maharashtra, Uttar Pradesh, Andhra Pradesh, Delhi, Jammu and Kashmir, Jharkhand and West Bengal and are suspected to have traveled to Iraq, Syria or Afghanistan to join the IS. [10] Those arrested were largely detained during the early stages of planning attacks and recruited online primarily by an Islamic State handler by the name of Shafi Armar (aka Yusuf-al-Hindi) based in Syria.

---

6 Abhishek Bhalla, "Islamic State using Indians against India, hiring Muslim youth to carry out local attacks," *Mail Today*, July 1, 2016, http://indiatoday.intoday.in/story/isis-hyderabad-nia-syria/1/705078.html, accessed on September 24, 2016.

7 The first Indian IS follower to be detained was a Bangalore-based youth found tweeting with the handle @ShamiWitness in support of the organisation. Among its fighters, Majeed was the first to be arrested when he arrived at the Mumbai airport six months after he traveled to the Islamic State. SudhiRanjan Sen, "How Alleged Islamic State Fighter ArifMajeed Was Brought Home to Mumbai," *NDTV*, November 28, 2014,http://www.ndtv.com/india-news/how-alleged-islamic-state-fighter-arif-majeed-was-brought-home-to-mumbai-705610 , accessed on July 22, 2016.

8 Milind Ghatwai, Praveen Swami, "First Islamic State 'module' busted, 5 held in MP: Police," *The Indian Express*, May 6, 2015, http://indianexpress.com/article/india/india-others/first-islamic-state-module-busted-5-held-in-mp-police/ , accessed on August 20, 2016.

9 Rajya Sabha, Question no. 2677 (Ministry of Home Affairs), Government of India, August 10, 2016.

10 Press Trust of India, "Rajya Sabha informed about 54 ISIS supporters arrested from country," *DNA*,August 11, 2016, http://www.dnaindia.com/india/report-rajya-sabha-informed-about-54-isis-supporters-arrested-from-country-2243859, accessed on October 10, 2016.

Visual evidence of Indian citizens within ISIS forces first emerged in July 2015 when the Islamic State's media wing, Al Hayat Media, posted images of two boats carrying about a dozen Indian nationals armed for battle. [11] A year later, the IS released its first recruitment video showcasing five Indian recruits who narrated their journey to the Islamic State, extolled the virtues of the IS way of life, urged Indian citizens to join their cause, and threatened to avenge atrocities committed against Muslims in India. [12] According to the Indian journalist Praveen Swami, this 22-minute documentary was the "first conclusive evidence that quite large numbers of Indians have in fact been drawn to jihadist groups fighting in West Asia… something large numbers are in denial about." [13]

Table 1. IS-linked arrests in India

(state-wise data presented in the Rajya Sabha on 04 May 2016, excluding Kerala)

S. No.	State-wise Breakdown	No. of IS-linked arrests
1	Telangana Police	06
2	Madhya Pradesh	05
3	Maharashtra Police	04
4	Delhi Police	04
5	Tamil Nadu Police	03
6	Karnataka Police	01
7	Rajasthan Police	01
8	Kerala Police* (till October 2016)	08

* Author's estimate

11 Sagnik Choudhury, "Islamic State video shows 'boatful of Indian' recruits, says one is dead IM man," *The Indian Express*, July 21, 2015, http://indianexpress.com/article/india/india-others/is-video-shows-boatful-of-indian-recruits-says-one-is-dead-im-man/ , accessed on September 15, 2016.

12 Praveen Swami, "Coming to avenge Babri, Muzaffarnagar, Gujarat, Kashmir: IS video," *The Indian Express*, May 25, 2016, http://indianexpress.com/article/india/india-news-india/avenge-babri-isis-video-islamic-state-indian-mujahideen-2811574/ , accessed on September 20, 2016.

13 Islamic State India Video: All You Need To Know, *The Indian Express*, May 24, 2016, https://youtu.be/Nw3urEozK_M, accessed on September 10, 2015.

The attack in Dhaka that killed twenty in June brought the threat closer to home. [14] In the Bangladeshi case, though the IS was quick to claim responsibility, closer investigation proved that local, known jihadi groups had aligned themselves with the IS to gain global notoriety. [15] The very same month in India, twenty-odd youngsters, including women and children, were reported missing by their families in the southern state of Kerala. This group had traveled to the IS province of Wilayat Khurasan.[16] Their recruiter, Sajeer Mangalachari Abdullah, remains at large at the time of writing and wanted for not only routing these followers but also for bringing together a second group of like-minded individuals in Kerala and directing them to conduct local 'lone-wolf' attacks. [17] These developments demand a critical discussion on the operational strategy of the IS to orchestrate attacks within India.

14 IANS, "Islamic State threat looms over India, can stage Dhaka like attacks: Agencies," *The Times of India*, July 3, 2016, http://economictimes.indiatimes.com/news/defence/islamic-state-threat-looms-over-india-can-stage-dhaka-like-attacks-agencies/articleshow/53029022.cms , accessed on September 25, 2016.

15 Press Trust of India, "Bangladesh police blames JMB for Dhaka cafe attack," *The Indian Express*, July 9, 2016, http://indianexpress.com/article/world/world-news/bangladesh-police-blames-jamaatul-mujahideen-bangladesh-jmb-for-dhaka-cafe-attack-2903911/ , accessed on September 21, 2016.

16 Shaju Philip, "21 missing in Kerala in a month: CM PinarayiVijayan in Assembly," *The Indian Express*, July 12, 2016, http://indianexpress.com/article/india/india-news-india/kerala-missing-muslim-youth-join-islamic-state-pinarayi-vijayan-cm-2908173/, accessed on October 12, 2016; "'I fight for Allah, I am a terrorist': Kerala's missing youngster's message to family?" *The Newsminute*, July 17, 2016, http://www.thenewsminute.com/article/i-fight-allah-i-am-terrorist-keralas-missing-youngsters-message-family-46638 , accessed on October 12, 2016; Ramesh Babu, Missing Kerala youth in Afghanistan, claim intelligence agencies," *Hindustan Times*, July 25, 2016, http://www.hindustantimes.com/india-news/missing-kerala-youth-in-afghanistan-claim-intelligence-agencies/story-AqYb8KD0Q0cqKYbdJvkIrK.html , accessed on October 12, 2016.

17 Praveen Swami, "Kerala man is key Islamic State 'recruiter' luring Indian volunteers to Afghanistan," *The Indian Express*, October 20, 2016, http://indianexpress.com/article/india/india-news-india/kerala-islamic-state-recruiter-indian-volunteers-afghanistan-isis-mosul-attack-3092431/, accessed on October 20, 2016.

Operational strategy and feeder groups

In its mouthpiece *Dabiq*, the Islamic State has made threats to avenge atrocities against Muslims in Kashmir, Gujarat, Assam and Mumbai as well as against the Indian Prime Minister Narendra Modi and all "pagan" Hindus in the country. The fighters in the video released in 2015 also declare the same, some even vowing to return to India to continue their fight.

From interviews of the regional commanders of *Wilayat Khurasan* (Afghanistan) and *Bengal* (Bangladesh) in the magazine, the IS' operational strategy for India becomes clearer. The plan relies on local Indian recruits to create the conditions necessary for an IS takeover – *"Bengal is located on the eastern side of India, whereas WilāyatKhurāsān is located on its western side. Thus, having a strong jihād base in Bengal will facilitate performing guerilla attacks inside India simultaneously from both sides and facilitate creating a condition of tawahhush (chaos) in India along with the help of the existing local mujahidin there..."* [18]

This strategy seems to be quietly underway in India. The Indian Mujahideen (IM), an indigenous terrorist organisation, has proved to be a useful feeder group to the IS. The IM gained notoriety in 2008 when it executed a series of terror attacks across India with the support of the Pakistan-based terror group the Lashkar-e-Taiba and their handlers, the Pakistani intelligence service (ISI). [19] The group has been unable to carry out attacks since 2013 after intelligence agencies cracked down hard on sleeper cells and modules nationwide and forced its leadership to flee to Pakistan.

Today, an IM splinter group – the Ansar-ut Tawhid fi Bilad al-Hind (Supporters of Monotheism in the Land of India) – is the one specifically

18 Interview with the Amir of the IS' Bengal faction, *Dabiq*, Issue 14, p. 63, https://azelin.files.wordpress.com/2016/04/the-islamic-state-22dacc84biq-magazine-1422.pdf , accessed on August 02, 2016.

19 The Islamic State's views on South Asian terrorist organisations like the Lashkar-e-Toiba (LeT) and the Al Qaeda in the Indian Subcontinent (AQIS) are quite negative as these groups are seen to be weak as they "proceed in accordance with the orders of the Pakistani intelligence." Sumitha Narayanan Kutty, "ISIS's Plan to Terrorize India, *The National Interest*, July 20, 2016, http://nationalinterest.org/feature/isiss-plan-terrorize-india-17052, accessed on August 4, 2016.

aligned with the IS in Iraq and Syria. This faction grew increasingly frustrated with the original leaders of the IM and their Pakistani handlers and moved to Afghanistan to gain combat experience. From here, they traveled to the IS territory in Iraq and Syria. This was confirmed by one of the Indian fighters featured in the propaganda video targeting India.

The leader of this faction, ShafiArmar or Yusuf-al-Hindi, is believed to lead the online recruitment of Indians and guides them on how to conduct strikes within India. Under Armar's command, the local operatives in India also organised themselves under the *Junud-ul-Khalifa-e-Hind* (Soldiers of the Indian Caliphate). The JKH gained a following after it became increasingly difficult for large groups of Indian fighters to travel to the Islamic State in Iraq and Syria without calling attention upon themselves.[20]

State Response

The Indian government banned the IS in December 2014 under the Unlawful Activities Prevention Act. [21] On the question of a military response in Iraq and Syria, Indian defence minister Manohar Parrikar expressed willingness to participate in operations only under the UN flag. [22] Consequently, India did not join the US-led 'Global Coalition' created to defeat ISIS in 2014.

'Police' and 'Public Order' are state subjects in India, i.e. respective state governments execute their own policies. The Central government therefore plays a supporting role to the various states in dealing with security issues such as terrorism. It has held at least two high-level meetings since August 2015 bringing together all Central agencies dealing with the IS threat and the 12-13 concerned state governments. The state governments have

20 There is very limited open source information on the JKH's structure and functioning.

21 Press Trust of India, "India bans Islamic State terror group," *The Hindu*, February 26, 2015, http://www.thehindu.com/news/national/india-bans-islamic-state-terror-group/article6937495.ece, accessed on August 5, 2016.

22 Press Trust of India, "India ready for operation against ISIS if UN adopts resolution: Manohar Parrikar," *The Economic Times*, December 16, 2015, http://economictimes.indiatimes.com/news/defence/india-ready-for-operation-against-isis-if-un-adopts-resolution-manohar-parrikar/articleshow/50199314.cms, accessed on August 15, 2016.

focused their attention on identifying potential recruits through cyber surveillance, taking further action against them when deemed necessary.

The Home Ministry's response to questions in parliament also details other measures by state governments, specifically "sharing and monitoring of information / intelligence with the field formations on real time basis, modernization of police force, installations of CCTV systems and electronic gadgets, effective and real time coordination among different wings of police, sensitizing police by way of regular training, introduction of visible policing and monitoring of social media etc." [23]

There seems to be some merit in this de-centralized approach, which hinges greatly on coordination not only among the various states but also between the Centre and the states. State police forces have thus adopted diverse responses toward their respective districts as they have a better grasp over its concerns. [24] Their approaches to individuals attempting to flee to IS territory have however had mixed results. [25]

Aside from internal coordination, the Indian government has spent the last year beefing up its intelligence-sharing mechanisms with strategic partners in the Middle East, most significantly the United Arab Emirates (UAE) and Saudi Arabia. At least a dozen Indian nationals have been deported from the UAE and arrested by the NIA for suspected links with the IS. [26] India is also working to expand its cooperation in this regard with Southeast Asian governments, particularly those experienced in dealing with jihadist networks, IS-inspired operations and de-radicalisation

23 Rajya Sabha, Starred Question no. 39 (Ministry of Home Affairs), Government of India, July 20, 2016.

24 Author's observation based on interviews with officers in the Kerala Police

25 For instance, the southern state of Telangana has adopted a counter-terrorism model (coined the 'Telangana model') that emphasizes counseling and deradicalization of individuals who were detained while attempting to join the IS in Iraq or Syria. Some detained youth however made multiple attempts to leave the country despite these efforts.

26 Press Trust of India, "3 Indian ISIS supporters deported from UAE, arrested by NIA," *India Today*, January 29, 2016, http://indiatoday.intoday.in/story/3-isis-sympathisers-arrested-by-nia-after-deported-from-uae/1/583266.html , accessed on August 20, 2016.

efforts. [27] The next section explores the Southeast Asian experience in greater detail.

Southeast Asia: Sanctuary in the Philippines

The biggest impact of the IS in the Southeast Asian region has been seen in the states of Indonesia, Malaysia and the Philippines. As indicated previously, around a thousand fighters in the Islamic State in Iraq and Syria belong to this group of countries. They pose a relatively small, but *real*, threat. This region has battled jihadist groups since the 1990s, catalyzed by fighters returning from the Afghan jihad against the Soviet Union. The returnees formed the core of the Jemaah lslamiah (JI) in Indonesia and Malaysia and the Abu Sayyaf group (ASG) in southern Philippines and engaged in several incidents of terrorism across the region. Though much of the Jemaah Islamiah was dismantled by 2009, the ASG successfully thrives in the Philippines even today.

The region's history with jihadist networks saw the Islamic State prioritise recruitment from Southeast Asia early on. The group targeted Indonesians and Malaysians with propaganda and training videos from 2014. A Malay-based combat unit, Katibah Nusantara, was established in September 2014 with about a hundred fighters from Indonesia and Malaysia. [28] The IS has released six videos since 2014, some originally in Bahasa and others with subtitles. In addition, IS magazine *Dabiq* has been available in Bahasa since its first edition. [29] The group also released its first propaganda video of a terror training camp in the jungles of Philippines in June this year.[30] The video instructed IS supporters in Southeast Asia to

27 Press Information Bureau, "India and Malaysia to proactively engage to combat the menace of ISIS," Ministry of Home Affairs, Government of India, July 18, 2016. http://pib.nic.in/newsite/PrintRelease.aspx?relid=147209, accessed on October 15, 2016.

28 Lim Yan Liang, "Countering the ISIS threat to Singapore and the region," *The Straits Times*, November 1, 2015, http://www.straitstimes.com/singapore/countering-the-isis-threat-to-singapore-and-the-region, accessed on October 10, 2016.

29 Remy Mahzam, "Children in ISIS Nusantara Media Outreach," *RSIS Commentary*, No. 166, 1 July 2016, https://www.rsis.edu.sg/rsis-publication/icpvtr/co16166-children-in-isis-nusantara-media-outreach/#.WA6kAJN95E4, accessed on October 5, 2016.

30 Raul Dancel, "ISIS targets South-east Asia radicals in latest recruitment video;

head to the Philippines. The Jakarta attack in January this year was the first IS-inspired strike. It was also the first attack that the Indonesian capital city had witnessed since 2009. Investigations concluded that this was an attack conducted by Indonesians within the country and directed by an Indonesian IS fighter in Syria. It exposed Indonesia's continuing problem with homegrown terrorism. [31]

Philippine Feeder Group: Abu Sayyaf Group

Certain members of the Abu Sayyaf Group (ASG) in the Philippines pledged their allegiance to the IS chief Abu Bakr al-Baghdadi in August 2014. [32] However, it was only in February 2016 that the IS core leadership officially recognised the group's pledge. It has since released an infographic depicting its presence in five different locations in the country, though an official caliphate has not yet been declared. This gap between the ASG's pledge and its acceptance gave credence to the argument that the ASG used the opportunity in 2014 to gain global publicity and further its own agenda, such as increasing the ransom demand for its foreign hostages. [33] One point to also note here is that the ASG has always practiced mutilation tactics, particularly beheadings, and thus fits seamlessly into IS' brand of brutality. There are established ideological links between the ASG and IS but operational ones are yet to be determined.

Security forces in the Philippines, however, refuse to acknowledge the influence of the Islamic State in their efforts to undermine the group's

'propaganda', says Philippines," *The Straits Times*, June 23, 2016, http://www.straitstimes.com/asia/se-asia/isis-targets-south-east-asia-radicals-in-latest-recruitment-video-propaganda-says, accessed on October 7, 2016.

31 Sara Schonhardt and I Made Sentana, Jakarta Attack Planner's Goal: A Leadership Role in Islamic State, *The Wall Street Journal*, January 15, 2016, http://www.wsj.com/articles/jakarta-attack-planners-goal-a-leadership-role-1452856415, accessed on October 16, 2016.

32 Agence France-Presse, "BIFF, Abu Sayyaf pledge allegiance to Islamic State jihadists," GMA News Online, August 16, 2014, http://www.gmanetwork.com/news/story/375074/news/nation/biff-abu-sayyaf-pledge-allegiance-to-islamic-state-jihadists, accessed October 21, 2016.

33 Michelle Florcruz, "Philippine Terror Group Abu Sayyaf May Be Using ISIS Link For Own Agenda," *International Business Times*, September 25, 2016, http://www.ibtimes.com/philippine-terror-group-abu-sayyaf-may-be-using-isis-link-own-agenda-1695156, accessed on October 18, 2016.

narrative in the region. This denial exists even as troops have doubled down on the ASG under President Duterte's orders. [34] The Philippine's neighbours fear that the IS is only a step away from declaring a *wilayat* in the country, which would make the country a sanctuary for its supporters in the region.

Table 2. Sampling of recent attacks (successful & foiled) in Southeast Asia

- **Indonesia**: Jakarta, 14 January 2016 – Five terrorists, including two suicide bombers, target police station and shopping district killing four civilians
- **Indonesia**: Solo, 5 July 2016 – IS supporter attacks a police station in the Central Java Province city, killing himself and injuring a policeman
- **Malaysia**: Selangor, 28 June 2016 – Two men threw a hand grenade at patrons of a night club in the outskirts of Kuala Lumpur injuring eight people
- **Indonesia/Singapore**: Batam, 5 August 2016 – Six arrested from the Indonesian island for planning a rocket attack on Singapore's iconic Marina Bay area
- **Philippines**: Davao, 2 September 2016: Bombing at night market kills 15, injures 70

Responses

Southeast Asian governments have uneven responses to the Islamic State problem. While Singapore, Indonesia and Malaysia have acknowledged the group's linkages to their local jihadist networks and begun decisive actions to dismantle them, the Philippine government and security apparatus refuse to acknowledge that the Islamic State holds any sway in its territory even as it cracks down on the ASG with renewed energy.

Malaysia, which repealed its Internal Security Act in 2012, passed a new Prevention of Terrorism Act (POTA) in 2015 to combat the transnational

34 Raul Dancel, "ISIS targets South-east Asia radicals in latest recruitment video; 'propaganda', says Philippines," *The Straits Times*, June 23, 2016, http://www.straitstimes.com/asia/se-asia/isis-targets-south-east-asia-radicals-in-latest-recruitment-video-propaganda-says, accessed on October 7, 2016.

threat posed by IS. The country established a de-radicalisation center and plans to open a counter-extremist messaging center later this year. Singapore has been promoting public awareness and safety and working to improve interagency coordination. Malaysia and Singapore have also contributed to the US-led Global Coalition to Counter ISIL. [35] Indonesia, in the meantime, is working to toughen its laws since it does not have a preventive detention mechanism currently.

There is a palpable need to step up the level of coordination between Indonesia, Malaysia and the Philippines, particularly in the waters in the tri-border area near the Philippine Sulu archipelago that includes the Malaysian state of Sabah and Indonesia's Sulawesi island. With air travel to Syria and Iraq restricted, IS recruits increasingly use sea routes to get to the Philippines. [36] The three governments have decided on joint sea patrols this year to combat piracy, human trafficking and terrorism related crimes, including kidnappings of their citizens by the ASG. [37]

Conclusion: Takeaways that Influence Response

From the above assessment of the Islamic State's appeal and capabilities in India and Southeast Asia, it is clear that the threat is essentially local and terrorist networks familiar. IS-inspired operatives rely on existing networks to conduct strikes and build explosive devices. [38]

35 PrashanthParameswaran, "ASEAN's Islamic State Conundrum," *The Diplomat*, October 20, 2016, http://thediplomat.com/2016/10/aseans-islamic-state-conundrum/, accessed on October 24, 2016.

36 *Reuters*, "Some Indonesians 'joining pro-Islamic State groups in Philippines'," *Channel News Asia*, October 25, 2016, http://www.channelnewsasia.com/news/asiapacific/some-indonesians-joining-pro-islamic-state-groups-in-philippine/3234136.html, accessed on October 25, 2016.

37 Marguerite AfraSapiie, "Indonesia to start joint sea patrols with Malaysia, Philippines," *The Jakarta Post*, August 2, 2016, http://www.thejakartapost.com/news/2016/08/02/indonesia-to-start-joint-sea-patrols-with-malaysia-philippines.html, accessed on October 17, 2016.

38 AzaanJavaid, "NIA recovers weapons, explosives, chemicals during raids of terror modules with alleged ISIS links," *DNA*, June 29, 2016, http://www.dnaindia.com/india/report-nia-recovers-weapons-explosives-chemicals-during-raids-of-terror-modules-with-alleged-isis-links-2229387 , accessed on October 3, 2016.

Second, given the limited resources and the urgency in devising strategies, it would prove helpful to central and state agencies to prioritize certain brackets of recruits in accordance with the threat levels they pose to the homeland. For instance, in India, three major categories of recruits are – (i) operatives active within India; (ii) fighters returning from IS-occupied territories; and (iii) individuals traveling abroad to IS territories. The most dangerous recruit is the one willing to stay behind to execute the organisation's ideology. Agencies have prioritized the detention of local IS operatives and the dismantling of their modules and sleeper cells. These busts provide vital clues to map out the current command structure and pinpoint their handlers in Iraq and Syria.

Third, the demonstrated operational capabilities of IS recruits in India and Southeast Asia (excluding the Philippines) have so far been limited. This could however change quickly if hardened, better-trained fighters return from Iraq and Syria to their home countries or relocate to vulnerable ones.

Fourth, the interrogation of IS-inspired recruits in India has revealed a network of associates based abroad in the Middle East. These external linkages seem to have provided vital financial support for IS-inspired operations in India. [39] Such links to the diaspora are also a major concern in Southeast Asia that has a large number of Indonesians, Malaysians and Filipinos residing in the Gulf States. [40]

Mapping this local landscape also leaves us with many questions that cannot as yet be addressed by the open source literature. For starters, the role of women in this organisation has been a very active one (even

---

39 According to the chargesheet filed by the NIA in one particular set of arrests, "funds were transferred by the accused persons from the UAE to the recipients from Tunisia, Philippines and India." There is relatively little data publicly available on the workings of India's anti-money laundering and counterterrorist financing laws, in particular its agreements with partner countries in the Middle East. Press Release, "Charge –sheet filed in ISIS conspiracy case," NIA, July 25, 2016, Ministry of Home Affairs, Government of India, http://www.nia.gov.in/writereaddata/Portal/News/85_1_PRESS_RELEASE_25_07_2016_2.pdf , accessed on October 1, 2016.

40 Aurea Calica, Noy: No terror threat in Phl amid Jakarta attack, *The Philippine Star*, January 16, 2016, http://www.philstar.com/headlines/2016/01/16/1543066/noy-no-terror-threat-phl-amid-jakarta-attack, accessed on October 10, 2016.

in India) and there is a need to better understand their involvement in the recruitment, fund raising and engagement in jihad. The transnational linkages between recruits, particularly in the case of Southeast Asia, are also understudied and a better understanding of these would help devise better transnational responses. [41]

As its territory shrinks, the IS has refocused its attention on its global allure. The group's spokesperson Abu Muhammad Al-Adnani declared in May this year, "The smallest action you do in their heartland is better and more enduring to us than what you would if you were with us." [42] In short, *go big but stay home*. Governments in India and South East Asia are right to worry that recruits have received this directive loud and clear. The counter-war for these countries has to rightly focus now on the Islamic State - the ideology, rather than the Islamic State - the territorial entity in Iraq and Syria.

41 "Pro-ISIS groups in Mindanao and their Links to Indonesia and Malaysia," IPAC Report No. 33, Institute for Policy Analysis of Conflict, October 25, 2016, http://file.understandingconflict.org/file/2016/10/IPAC_Report_33.pdf, accessed on October 25, 2016.

42 Maher Chmaytelli, Stephen Kalin and Ali Abdelaty, "Islamic State calls for attacks on the West during Ramadan in audio message," Reuters, May 22,2016, http://www.reuters.com/article/us-mideast-crisis-islamicstate-idUSKCN0YC0OG, accessed on October 15, 2016; Pamela Engel, "ISIS just delivered its 'weakest message' ever," *Business Times*, May 24, 2016, http://www.businessinsider.sg/isis-adnani-message-2016-5/#St1IYQg7AysJmIWf.97, accessed on August 14, 2016.

Non-Traditional Security Challenges in the Indo-Pacific Region: Prospects for Cooperation

Victor Sumsky

The concept of non-traditional security challenges (NTSCs) is a product of the early post-Cold War era. This period was marked by a general assumption that traditional challenges and threats associated with great power rivalries and global military clashes should not be a matter of concern in a unipolar world dominated by just one, presumably benign superpower.

The more or lesscanonic list of NTSCs that has emerged since then, includes natural disasters, climate change, new diseases, food and water shortages, transnational crime (such as human trafficking and drug trafficking), piracy, terrorism and cybercrime.

Curiously, of all the phenomena mentioned above only cybercrime can be viewed as something truly non-traditional. The rest of them are modern day variations on themes as old as our planet itself (if we talk about natural disasters and climate change) or as old as the human race and social strife (in practically all the other cases).

In retrospect, it is tempting to suggest that, from the Cold War winners' perspective, the notion of NTSCs was a great invention. It justified the continued existence of huge military formations, saved hordes of generals, security analysts and scientists from untimely retirement, and added a humanizing touch to the global policeman image of the only superpower.

As time goes, it becomes more and more clear that it is not possible to sustain unipolarity while responding adequately to what we habitually call non-traditional challenges. Just look at how, against the backdrop of alarmist climate change rhetoric, climatic weaponry is being developed (and, quite probably, tested). Take into account that bringing electronic espionage to previously unthinkable levels was a major single motive for creating Internet, and acknowledge that cyber-counterattacks have been a natural and predictable response to this challenge. See how the practice of humanitarian interventions (which is an extension of the NTSCs discourse) invariably results in the rise of terrorism where previously there was none.

In spite of all the attention given by academics and security practitioners to NTSCs, the latter are rather increasing than decreasing. The process of studying them and dealing with them has been so heavily permeated with purely traditional motives (such as the urge to secure global dominance) that the term starts to sound like a mockery. This impression is especially strong at the time of renewed great power tensions.

Why the kinds of tensions which were not supposed to re-emerge are here again? The answer has to do with an ongoing global shift towards multi-polarity. It was already under way during the late Cold War era. Once this era was over, the process continued under the guise of uni-polarity in a step-by-step fashion – until a few years ago accumulated quantitative change, as Marxists would put it, produced a qualitative leap. Early in the second decade of this century the evolutionary phase of transition towards multi-polarity has given way to a confrontation over this issue. What we see now is a situation approximating a zero-sum-game: while one party refuses to tolerate any further movement towards the multipolar world, the other one insists on proceeding in that direction and refuses to succumb to severe external pressure.

Today all sorts of overlapping challenges and threats are reinforcing each other in different parts of the world. This is anything but a spontaneous, unguided, impersonal process, and its consequences are disastrous. The darkest of these tragedies is unfolding on the Middle Eastern flank of the Indo-Pacific space. ISIS/Daesh and the likes of it would have never been able to hold their ground in Syria without the massive and coordinated help provided by professional global subversives – media operators, financiers, strategists and, ultimately, high governmental officials. So much for terrorism as the exemplary non-traditional threat.

The fiercely expansionist nature of ISIS/Daesh is in full harmony with its backers' passion for playing games on the Grand Chessboard. This alone is a sign that if the terrorists have the upper hand in Syria, the implications will be felt beyond its borders. If so, how far it might go and how big might be the damage? To do justice to this problem, one may need to view it in the geopolitical context of the Indo-Pacific space.

It has been stated by Moscow more than once that Russia as a supporter of Bashar Al-Assad's government and a staunch opponent of ISIS/Daesh is determined to pre-empt the advance of the latter in the direction of Caucasus and Central Asia. Does it mean that in Syria the Russians are protecting just their immediate periphery and national interests? Those who respond in the affirmative must be reminded that by gaining a foothold in Central Asia the terrorists (and their backers, of course) will be able to create problems not for Russia alone but for India and China as well.

If only ISIS/Daesh is allowed to expand in the directions outlined above, it is likely to create more than simply internal problems for the key proponents of the multipolar world. It might as well put in jeopardy a whole set of their regional and trans-regional initiatives, including China's One Belt One Road plan. What might be delayed due to this turn of events is the growth of the multipolar world's economic base. Or, in other words, the coming of the Age of Asia as opposed to the New American Century.

The strong emphasis on the counter-terrorism theme in the Declaration adopted by the 8th BRICS Summit in Goa is an encouraging sign of consensus within this grouping on the need to defeat the terrorists - in Syria and elsewhere - before it is too late.

PART – II

Economic Challenges and Prospects

Geopolitics of Energy Resources in the Indo-Pacific Region

Ms Shebonti Ray Dadwal

In recent times, four or five issues have brought the focus on the Indo-Pacific region. Divided into three sub-divisions, the Indo-Pacific stretches from the Gulf of Aden in the western part of the Indian Ocean, through the Red Sea, the Persian Gulf, the Arabian Sea, the Bay of Bengal and the Andaman Sea to the South China Sea, the Philippine Sea, the East China Sea and the seas surrounding New Guinea to the western Pacific region. It hosts half of world population making it a huge market; many of the countries belong to the world's fastest growing economies; the region has huge hydrocarbon resources and critical minerals, particularly offshore, and finally, the most important transport corridors, both at sea as well as on land, transit through this region.

With regard to energy resources specifically, in the east, the South China Sea is potentially rich in hydrocarbons while several areas of the Indian Ocean too are believed to hold large reserves. As in the case of India, much of the offshore areas both in the Indian Ocean as well as the Western Pacific are under- or un-explored, with little or no thorough exploration work having been done. At the same time, the coastal beach sands and offshore waters of the Indian Ocean are believed to hold large deposits of critical mineral elements such as rare earth, as well as marine life that are increasingly important for both exports and domestic consumption. As a result, over the last few decades, because of its fast-paced economic growth, the region, which is now increasingly been referred to as Indo-Pacific, is also the largest consumer of energy to sustain growth rates, it has also emerged as the largest energy consumer – China, India, Japan, South Korea and the Southeast Asian states.

It should therefore come as no surprise that the region has become the epicenter of the global economy, with some of the largest markets, both for general trade as well trade in energy resources. It is also the reason why it has become the cynosure of global geopolitics, with the regional and extra-regional powers competing and/or collaborating with one another to expand their own influence as well as counter the influence of potential rivals. An obvious instance is when the US initiated its 'Rebalance to Asia' policy. It not only raised concerns in China, but also in many of the Persian Gulf states who feared that a lowering of the US' presence in the region would increase their vulnerability. Although the US has tried to reassure these states that it would not withdraw from the region, it has nevertheless seen a reordering of the traditional international security order, with huge consequences.

Adding to the oil exporting countries' concerns is the massive transformation that has taken place in the oil and gas markets. A combination of the fracking revolution and Iran's imminent return to the global oil market, the oil exporting countries dispensed with their traditional strategy of cutting production in order to retain - and even extend - their market share(s), resulting in an increase in the supply of oil and gas in the international energy market, which in turn led to a crash in oil - and gas - prices.

While the fall in prices has benefited the oil and gas importing countries, by reducing their energy import bills, it has also seen consumption increase in these countries. Already large hydrocarbon consumers, countries in Asia and the Pacific have seen their consumption of oil increasing twice as fast. But with less than 4 per cent of the world's proven oil reserves, the region has few options to increase or even maintain current levels of domestic production, and efforts to diversify to other types of energy, such as natural gas or renewable energy resources, have achieved only limited success. Now, with the price of oil and gas at an all-time low, their dependence on energy imports has grown incrementally.

As a result, by 2030, the region is expected to be the world's largest consumer of hydrocarbons. In the next 5-10 years, around 300 billion barrels of oil will need to be developed and brought to market and, according to most analysts, by 2025 Asian demand for LNG will double. As a result, while today these countries are benefiting from the low energy prices, over the long term it will have negative consequences. Not only will more use of fossil fuels lead to an increase in carbon emissions, the fall in prices will discourage investments in new production, eventually leading to a price escalation, albeit not as low as witnessed in 2014-15.

Secondly, as the region grows in importance, concerns over the safety of its sea lanes of communication, or SLOCS, are increasing. In the South China Sea, roughly one third of the global oil trade and about half that of global gas (LNG) supplies transit through these waters and the chokepoints of the Straits of Malacca, Sunda and Lombok. According to the US Department of Energy, these sea lanes account for roughly 75-80 per cent of China 's oil imports, 85-90 per cent of Japan's and South Korea's oil imports, and 33 per cent of Japan's and South Korea's LNG imports.[1] Moreover, Australia is likely to become the world's largest LNG exporter by 2020, and the vast majority of its LNG exports will pass through the South China Sea to markets in East Asia and India, while Singapore's role as a major refining hub supplying oil products throughout Asia is also dependent on open and secure sea lanes. India is also a major refining centre and exporter of oil products to East Asia through the South China Sea.

In the Indian Ocean, the Strait of Hormuz sees about 90 per cent of the oil exports from the Persian Gulf transit through these waters each day, carrying more than 18 per cent of the world's oil demand. But now, with the US' reliance on oil and gas imports declining due to the fracking revolution that has taken place in North America, there are concerns whether the US Navy will remain as invested in ensuring the safety of these shipping routes and chokepoints.

At the same time, the US' pivot to Asia has increased Beijing's concerns regarding the safety of its sea-based trade. With 82 per cent of its oil imports passing through these waters, China's sense of vulnerability to any disruptions in supplies has grown with the US' renewed interest in the region. Despite attempts at reducing its dependency on the Malacca Strait by increasing its energy imports through overland pipelines from Central Asia, Russia, Myanmar, and more recently through Pakistan via Gwadar, the majority of China's oil imports, which are sourced from West

1 Mikkal Herberg, The Role of Energy in Disputes over the South China Sea, Maritime Awareness Program, June 28, 2016, http://maritimeawarenessproject.org/2016/06/28/the-role-of-energy-in-disputes-over-the-south-china-sea/

Asia as well as Africa, continue to be sea-based. As a result, it has tried to establish and extend its jurisdiction and influence in the region by claiming sovereignty over huge swathes of the South China Sea, including the Spratly and Paracel Islands, which are also claimed by some of the other Southeast Asian states. These conflicting territorial claims, which have long stoked tensions, have increased after China commenced constructing artificial islands in the area. For instance, even as relations between China and Japan deteriorate, Beijing's aggressive stance in the South China Sea has increased Tokyo's concerns about an expanded Chinese military presence in the area. Like China, it too depends on these waters for 85-90 per cent of its oil imports and 33 per cent of its LNG imports.[2]

Moreover, according to some analysts, apart from ensuring free and unhindered passage through the sea lanes, the presence of hydrocarbon resources are also a factor of conflict in the region. China has been seeking to exploit the areas in Reed Bank, which is located off the Philippines coast, for billions of barrels of oil as well as gas, and according to reports in the Philippines media, it was set to enter into an agreement with Manila to explore for the same.[3]Although there are conflicting data with regard to the exact reserves of oil and gas in the region, the US Geological Survey estimates that the South China Sea region holds some 11 billion barrels of oil and 190 trillion cubic feet of natural gas reserves. The China National Offshore Oil Company (CNOOC), which is the state-owned offshore energy exploration company, states a much higher figure of around 125 billion barrels of oil and 500 trillion cubic feet of natural gas.

China has also challenged Vietnam's offshore deep water exploration activity, including the joint projects with India's ONGC, Russia's Gazprom and Exxon Mobil and in 2014, CNOOC had even begun drilling in waters claimed by Hanoi, leading to violent demonstrations in Vietnam and attacks on Chinese businesses.

2 ReinhardDrifte, "Japan's Policy towards the South China Sea – Applying "Proactive Peace Diplomacy"?, Peace Research Institute Frankfurt (PRIF) Report No. 140, 2016, http://www.hsfk.de/fileadmin/HSFK/hsfk_publikationen/prif140.pdf

3 Clay Dillow, "US on edge over new powder keg in the South China Sea", CNBC, October 21, 2016,http://www.cnbc.com/2016/10/21/china-and-the-philippines-could-ink-oil-exploration-deal-in-south-china-sea.html

All these tensions has seen the South China Sea region turning into a potentially zone of conflict, which in turn has impacted on the development of new oil and gas resources in the majority of the South China Sea, particularly in what could be the deeper-water areas.

Therefore, it is important to explore ways of addressing resource exploitation, even if sovereignty claims remain unresolved. While maritime order is underpinned by the international law of the sea, primarily based on UNCLOS, there are still several instances of unilateral attempts to change the status quo by coercion.

Secondly, with growing concerns over climate change, and the attempt by several of these nations to shift to cleaner and renewable energy resources, the demand for critical minerals, including rare earth elements that are required for the manufacture of high-technology products required for clean energy applications, as well as for other products used in sectors like aerospace, automobiles, cameras, defence, entertainment systems, laptops, medical imaging, nuclear energy, and smartphones, too will increase. India, as well as most of the Asian countries, do not possess, or do not have the capacity to produce, these critical minerals and are 100 per cent dependent on the import of many of these minerals. With China holding the bulk of many of these critical minerals, concerns over dependence on Beijing for these critical minerals are rising. It would bear remembering that in 2010, China cut its exports of rare earth minerals used in products like hybrid cars, wind turbines and guided missiles to Japan following a dispute over Japan's detention of a Chinese fishing trawler captain. As a result, in 2011, when the International Sea Bed Authority's (ISBA's) decided to allow the China Ocean Mineral Resources Research and Development Association (COMRA) to undertake exploration for poly-metallic sulphides in a 10,000 square km area in the south-west Indian Ocean that were over and above its existing allocation in the Western Pacific, the Indian strategic community saw this as an attempt to extend China's footprint in the Indian Ocean Region.

Although China has said it was open to the joint development of energy reserves in the South China Sea, other states have been wary as they fear that China will use its economic leverage to strengthen its claims over the disputed areas. A recent example is the Philippines case, where under the current President Rodrigo Duterte's predecessor, Manila had challenged China's claim at the Permanent Court of Arbitration at The

Hague and won, Beijing refused to accept the decision. The contentious nature of the disputes has been a key sticking point in the search for a collective solution to the region's energy security problems, resulting in a distinct lack of trust and regional consensus.

Nevertheless, there have been significant attempts to regionalize resource cooperation. In the last decade, various inter-governmental bodies, including ASEAN, ASEAN+3, and the East Asia Summit, launched several energy cooperation initiatives that were aimed at further integration of national resource markets. However, while most of these initiatives have been successful in improving dialogue and information sharing, they have not resulted in any major changes as the various governments have remained highly conscious of protecting their sovereignty over decision-making and wary of liberalization initiatives.

What then needs to be done to ensure that the region's energy requirements are secured?

First, there is therefore an urgent need to develop supply, and the long cycle time of developing supply. Although the region also holds great promise as an energy supplier, the countries in the Indo-Pacific region remain net energy importers, by and large.

Second, all countries should agree to adhere to a rules-based international order and peaceful settlements of territorial disputes through negotiations rather than taking unilateral action. In this regard, the need for supporting open sea lanes, not only for general trade but also for their energy security, is crucial. While maritime order is supported by the international law of the sea, primarily based on UN Convention on the Law of the Sea or UNCLOS, there are several instances where unilateral action has attempted to change the status quo by coercion.

Third, although the US is the main 'policeman' in the world's vital sea lanes, it cannot be expected to carry the burden alone. It is time to see whether other nations can also share the burden of patrolling the SLOCs, without raising concerns of regional nations.

With regard to energy specifically, there is an urgent need for all countries to forego their inward-looking and individualistic stances with regard to energy markets as the best guarantor of energy security is open and transparent energy markets. Viewing the emerging energy scenario from the perspective of individual requirements will in the long term exacerbate an already tenuous situation.

State-owned companies could enter into more joint ventures in energy exploration and production (E&P), as well as refineries and retail operations, as well as development of infrastructure, such as pipelines, ports, and terminals, in cooperation with private sector oil producers.

Second, with regard to transiting critical sea lanes, the possibility of alternative sea routes along with ways to improve security in the chokepoints through joint patrols, study potential pipeline routes, etc. should be looked at. For example, the recent expansion of the Panama Canal has allowed the US to gain a huge advantage in transporting larger volumes more economically to the East Asian markets. Similar routes can be studied in the Indo-Pacific region and the Indian Ocean region.

Third, revisit the idea of holding joint strategic petroleum reserves (SPRs), to be released to member countries in times of supply crises or price spikes, as it would assist some of the poorer countries in alleviating the high cost of maintaining the SPRs.

Create a truly Asian energy market with Asian pricing benchmarks, particularly for gas. An initial attempt by the 4 Asian consumers (India, China, SK and Japan) did not take off due to the fall in oil and gas prices. It is time to have a relook at this initiative.

Finally, given the big challenges faced by the international energy scene in recent years such as market turbulence, climate change concerns and renewed focus on sustainable energy access, interest in the global energy dialogue is strong and rising as all parties strive to better understand the complexities of the evolving energy landscape. There is a greater awareness of the common challenges facing energy producing, consuming and transit countries, as well as the industry stakeholders.

What is sorely lacking but is imperative, are global energy governance rules. Global cooperation is needed to address these various challenges, specifically to share information, to agree norms, rules and standards, and to put in place appropriate economic instruments such as carbon pricing or emissions trading and to promote better governance at national levels, by putting in place systems to reduce corruption and rent seeking and enhance transparency through instruments like the Extractive Industries

Transparency Initiative (EITI). Moreover, providing physical security of energy infrastructure against such threats as terrorism and climate change also requires global coordination in some instances.

Unfortunately, efforts to promote producer-consumer energy cooperation in the Indo-Pacific region have similarly failed to live up to expectations.

The existing institutions like the International Energy Agency (IEA), the International Energy Forum (IEF), etc. are not trusted by some countries. Some governments have recommend setting up an energy governance forum under the G20. There are some positives and negatives in the suggestions. However, what is required is that some thinking is needed on this subject urgently before the global energy scenario gets even more contentious and critical.

The Indo-Pacific region carries a particularly heavy traffic of petroleum and petroleum products from the oilfields of the Persian Gulf and Indonesia. Its fish are of great and growing importance to the bordering countries for domestic consumption and export. Fishing fleets from Russia, Japan, South Korea, and Taiwan also exploit the Indian Ocean, mainly for shrimp and tuna. Large reserves of hydrocarbons are being tapped in the offshore areas of Saudi Arabia, Iran, India, and Western Australia. An estimated 40 percent of the world's offshore oil production comes from the Indian Ocean. Beach sands rich in heavy minerals and offshore placer deposits are actively. Coastal beach sands and offshore waters host heavy mineral deposits, and fisheries are increasingly important for both exports and domestic consumption.

Amidst the drive to maintain economic growth, energy security concerns are spiraling. Although currently the oil and gas market is over-supplied, market fundamentals will kick in in a few years and demand will exceed supply unless investment in production is sustained. From all accounts, this is not happening due to the nature of the oil and gas upstream sector as low oil and gas prices have seen investment in new production tapering off. Already the price of oil has started rising and Asian LNG prices that are oil-indexed will follow suit, albeit not in the near future.

The centre of gravity for the global energy system is shifting towards Asia. Conversely, Asia's economic growth is underpinned by energy supply, and energy security: First, the scale of demand growth of energy in this region; Second, the need to ensure adequate supply; and third, the role of energy partnerships to provide the supplies needed to meet the growing demand.

Growing economies and rising standards of living in the region have made this an area of focus for new energy markets. Demand for affordable energy in the region will only continue to grow so much so that by 2030, the region is expected to be the world's largest consumer of hydrocarbons. In the next five to ten years, around 300 billion barrels of oil will need to be developed and brought to market and, according to most analysts by 2025 Asian demand for LNG will double. The scale of the challenge is also reinforced by the anticipated global rates of production declines, with massive investment required just to be able to sustain current production.

Therefore there is an urgent need to develop supply, and the long cycle time of developing supply. Although the region also holds great promise as an energy supplier Asia stands today as a net energy importer. It has abundant energy resources and geothermal and fossil fuels, including abundant resources of natural gas that can be converted to LNG and transported around the region. The South China Sea is potentially resource rich by some estimates: 2.5 billion barrels of oil, and 25 trillion cubic feet of gas.

This brings us to the issue of the security of sea lanes, which are vital in transporting energy supplies from other areas of the world. The South China Sea – which has been a source of tension in recent times, is an essential transit area for the oil and gas, with the majority of imported supplies passing through just four narrow chokepoints, including the Malacca Strait, Sunda Strait, Philippine Sea, and Lombok Strait. As a result of its geographical location, reliance on imports and the current tensions in the South China Sea, between China on the one hand and other southeast Asian and East Asian states like Japan on the other, the region's collective energy security is looking increasingly vulnerable. Roughly one-third of the global oil trade and over one-half of global liquefied natural gas (LNG) trade passes through the South China Sea. According to the U.S. Department of Energy, these sea lanes account for roughly 75-80 percent of China's oil imports, 85 percent–90 percent of Japan's and South Korea's oil imports, and 33 percent of Japan's and South Korea's LNG imports. Moreover, Australia is likely to become the world's largest LNG exporter by

2020, and the vast majority of its LNG exports will pass through the South China Sea to markets in China, Japan, South Korea and India. Singapore's role as a major refining hub supplying oil products throughout Asia is also dependent on open and secure sea lanes. India is also a major refining centre and exporter of oil products to East Asia through the South China Sea.

Hence, securing reliable energy supplies and shipping to fuel Asia's prosperity is tightly bound up with the maintenance of freedom of navigation through the South China Sea and Malacca Strait and is a core energy and national security interest for virtually every regional power. The intensifying engagement between the People's Liberation Army (PLA) Navy and the U.S. Navy over navigational rights and the application of the United Nations Convention on the Law of the Sea (UNCLOS) in the South China Sea has significant energy security implications. China's island-building activity in the Spratlys, attempts strengthen its positions and claims in the Paracel Islands, and increasingly vocal assertions that these "islands" confer rights to 12 nautical mile territorial waters and potentially to EEZs of up to 200 nautical miles, if allowed to stand, would significantly undermine the existing U.S.-led architecture for maintaining open and unconstrained sea lanes throughout the South China Sea. China has tried to reassure the region that its presence in the region would help ensure freedom of navigation, but its interpretation of what rights maritime shipping and naval vessels would have within its territorial seas and EEZs seem to represent a narrower and potentially troubling interpretation of UNCLOS. Further, Beijing's "slow-walking" of negotiations for an ASEAN Code of Conduct and refusal to engage in the arbitral case brought by the Philippines add to suspicions about China's real intentions.

Hence, in order to reduce dependence on politically unstable countries, states are beginning to look closer to home for new energy reserves -particularly in offshore zones in the South China Sea, where there are projected to be several billion barrels of oil (up to 213 billion barrels of oil according to some estimates), along with extensive natural gas reserves. But overlapping and unresolved territorial claims have based on historical rights and international law has made any attempt by a country a contentious issue. An example is China has suggested joint development of energy reserves in the South China Sea; other states have been wary as a result of the unresolved territorial disputes, fearful of China furthering its economic leverage to strengthen their claims. The disputes (involving China, Vietnam, the Philippines, Taiwan, Malaysia and Brunei) consist of multiple, complex, and overlapping claims based on historical rights and international law. The contentious nature of the disputes has been a key sticking point in the search for a collective solution to the region's energy security problems, resulting in a distinct lack of trust and regional consensus.

Despite these divisions, there have been significant attempts to regionalize resource cooperation in order to achieve mutual benefits for the Asia-Pacific as a whole. During the last decade, various intergovernmental bodies such as ASEAN, ASEAN+3, and the East Asia Summit have launched energy cooperation initiatives aimed at further integration of national resource markets, with differing degrees of success. In general, these attempts have been successful in improving dialogue and information sharing, but have not resulted in any substantial changes. Governments have generally taken a more inward-looking approach, remaining highly conscious of protecting their sovereignty over decision making and wary of liberalization initiatives. At present, the largest barrier to greater energy cooperation comes in the form of the on-going territorial disputes in the South China Sea, which have made joint exploration extremely difficult and have discouraged international companies from becoming involved in projects in disputed waters.

Therefore, it is important to explore ways of addressing resource exploitation, even if sovereignty claims remain unresolved. While maritime order is underpinned by the international law of the sea, primarily based on UNCLOS, there are still several instances of unilateral attempts to change the status quo by coercion.

What type of security does the oil market, or the seaborne energy market, really need? Like to make 3 points, the three sensitive and important naval areas for Asian energy supply, you have the Strait of Hormuz, the Strait of Malacca – of Malacca and Singapore, and the South China Sea. So we take them in reverse: the South China Sea does not really present any threat to shipping. Most of the threats to shipping security are close to the shore, so you look at the Straits of Hormuz and the Straits of Malacca and Singapore.

On the other side, the Strait of Hormuz is equally important for the Asian economies. About 90 percent of the oil exports from the Persian Gulf transit the Strait of Hormuz each day - generally more than 17 million barrels or more than 18 percent of daily worldwide oil demand. But the US reliance on international trade in oil declining fast now, is it time for the Asian powers and local states, to take on a more important role in the security provision?

The best guarantor of energy security is open and transparent energy markets, and secondly without open sea lanes, there can be no energy security for any of us. Since it plays a key role in facilitating trade and oil flows, the Indo-Pacific is the principal theatre of geo-strategic competition between established and emerging powers.

Though experts say the probability of military conflict between China and India remains low, escalated activities (such as port development and military exercises) and rhetoric could endanger stability in a critical region for global trade flows. But the diverse non-traditional security challenges in the Indian Ocean Region (IOR) also offer areas of potential collaboration for China and India, as well as other regional actors.

In 2011, when the International Sea Bed Authority's (ISBA's) decided to allow the China Ocean Mineral Resources Research and Development Association (COMRA) to undertake exploration for poly-metallic sulphides in a 10,000 sq. kms area in the south-west Indian Ocean it caused a flutter in the Indian strategic community, which saw the development as a geo-strategic gambit aimed at extending China's footprint in the Indian Ocean Region (IOR).

What did not draw much attention then was the fact that the COMRA's exploration rights in the Indian Ocean were over and above its existing allocation in the Western Pacific. A 15-year contract with the seabed authority in 2001 had given China rights to explore 75,000 sqkms of seabed for poly-metallic nodules (small rocks containing metal ore – manganese, copper, cobalt, etc) in which it has shown rapid progress in extracting the minerals.

This is significant because ISBA's 2011 decision resulted in China establishing mining rights in two major oceanic systems that contain the world's most important sea lines of communication. To be sure, China's deep-sea exploration rights weren't apparently acquired through any backroom manoeuvres or use of geo-strategic clout. The license to explore the Western Indian Ocean sea-bed was, in major part, attributable to a concerted effort at scouting the seas and gathering evidence for the presence of mineral nodes on the sea bed. In fact, China's mining rights in the IOR were given six years after a Chinese government-sponsored expedition team found clues of an enormous belt of poly-metallic sulphides in a deep-sea rift south of Madagascar.

China and its assertive foreign policy has created geo-strategic flux in the Indo-Pacific region, which poses serious military, economic and political challenges to the US interests in the region. China's rise is swiftly altering the geo-strategic equations in the region. Its assertive foreign policy, backed by growing economic and military power, has also changed the geo-economics and geopolitics of the region. Though China's rise has benefited regional countries in the economic field, its increasing expenditure on military modernisation and power projection, particularly in the East and South China Seas, have caused major concerns.

With the rise of Asian economies, their growing dependence on Asian energy, with the emergence of Africa as the new continent of economic growth and the eastward turn of both Africa and West Asia, as they sell more of their resources to Asia rather than the West, the centre of gravity of global commerce has shifted from the Atlantic to what is now described as the 'Indo-Pacific'. Consequently, the Indian Ocean has again become the crossroads of global commerce.

Energy security is an important aspect of India's maritime economy and strategy and a key determinant of its Indian Ocean strategy. Of all the trade links that India has with the Indian Ocean region none is more important than the trade in oil and gas. India's economic rise has increased its dependence on imported energy. Not only is the import of crude oil increasingly important for the Indian economy, but also the export of refined petroleum and petroleum products. While India seeks to become more self-reliant in energy by developing nuclear and renewable energy, it will continue to be a major consumer of imported hydrocarbons and exporter of petroleum products. Hence, India has no option but to depend on the Indian Ocean to access its energy needs. Moreover, apart from West and Central Asia, India is also sourcing and investing in oil and gas exploration in South-east Asia and East Africa. All this imparts a strategic dimension to India's trade dependence on the Indian Ocean.

With the share of trans-Atlantic trade in world trade declining, the trans-Pacific remaining static and the share of Indian Ocean trade growing, ensuring freedom of access and movement into and out of the Indian Ocean, through its various entry and exit points known as 'chokepoints' is essential not just for the stability and security of India and Asia, but also for the stability and sustainability of global trade and economic growth. Moreover, the Indian Ocean is not just the crossroads of the world and the centre of gravity of the global economy but it is also a rich depository of marine resources, including minerals, oil and gas, fisheries and marine life.

Therefore, as the global economic weight shifts towards the region in coming years, and geopolitical relations within the region are reformed, concerns over access to energy and raw materials will increase. This can lead to resource nationalism and potential conflict over control of resources.

China's Belt and Road Initiative - Challenges and Prospects

Dr. Huang Yunsong

It is a great honor for me to be invited again to the annual international seminar of USI. I want to thank you for your hospitality and great efforts in organizing this wonderful event. This international platform created by USI is for professionals and scholars to deliberate on the key issues of the day. It is my hope that this seminar would facilitate to narrow our difference, if there's any, and enhance the consensus, which we actually need a lot.

I am glad to join in the second session, and share my observations on "China's Belt and Road Initiative - Challenges and Prospects". Instead of elaborating this topic in a general sense, I'd like to emphasize on OBOR within the specific context of South Asia, by revealing the conundrum in geopolitical interpretation of OBOR and its economic consequences.

Does anyone in the audience still feel interested in President Xi Jinping's One Belt One Road Initiative? To many of you, interested maybe, but most probably in a negative sense. This plan was to focus China's production capacity, monetary capital, and infrastructure assets, etc. along the traditional trading routes leading to Europe. Its potential impact upon the geopolitical status quo in South Asia remains uncertain. This was one of the reasons India, understandably, became deeply concerned about expansion of Chinese footprints on the Subcontinent, from Nepal in the north, to Sri Lanka in the south, from Bangladesh in the east, to Pakistan in the west.

Well, the One Belt One Road has been experiencing some head-on blows in the region for the past three years or so, due to strong opposition from certain players. Chinese Government not only had to adapt to the indifferent response from the Indian side, but also kept itself busy in overcoming setbacks in various forms in other South Asian partner states. When China was forced into a position to re-examine and adjust the initiative, it is very necessary to look through the lens of sceptics, in particular, the Indian policy makers and analysts.

Unilateralism Not Beijing's Approach

Unilateralism is so far India's official perspective on Beijing's approach toward connectivity in South Asia and its periphery, which was clearly stated in the literatures and comments made by the Indian Government, officials and strategic community.

When commenting on OBOR in this March during Raisina Dialogue, Foreign Minister Sushma Swaraj notably stressed: We bring to bear a *cooperative* rather than "*unilateral* approach" and believe that creating an environment of trust and confidence is the pre-requisite for a more inter-connected world.

Last year in Singapore, when asked about OBOR, Foreign Secretary Jaishankar, noted that it was not incumbent on other countries to necessarily buy into such "unilateral initiatives". He dismissed One Belt One Road as merely a national initiative devised with national interest, implying its negligence of the interests that an international or regional initiative should have. What Secretary Jaishankar is expecting is a larger discussion for larger buy in.

In this regard, I am very keen to reflect on the classic definition of this term in the field of foreign policy. Unilateralism is any doctrine or agenda that supports *one-sided action*. Such action may be in disregard for other parties, seeks no cooperation with or approval by other states. U.S. invasion of Iraq in 2003 was a textbook example of unilateralism, without support from the United Nations or even its allies. However, the accusation of OBOR as an approach of unilateralism was not very well grounded. Strictly speaking, the initiative is neither unilateral nor multilateral for many reasons.

Firstly, the rhetoric in the dispute between multilateralism and unilateralism ignores a fact that there are few policy decisions that are purely one or the other. Because in both approaches, national interests usually play the most crucial role in concluding a transnational initiative, one state canal ways rally a group of partner states, and one state often will not go completely alone to pursue its agenda. In my perception, a litmus test of an initiative of multilateralism should be the combination of common interests and voluntariness of relevant states. In that sense, OBOR is more of multilateralism, instead of unilateralism.

Secondly,OBOR is all but *one-sided action*, the very basis of which rests upon the approval by and the cooperation with the participating states. Moreover, Chinese entrepreneurs, engineers and investors serving the OBOR initiative are completely acting under the framework and the individual agreements jointly worked out by the undertakers from China and the participating states, and are also subject to the laws and regulations in place. In comparison with political and military agendas, I see very little room for China to enforce so called one-sided action in OBOR's implementation. It's just too hard to be true. If it's really one-sided and unilateral in absence of consent and support from the partner states, the chance for China to materialize OBOR would be zero.

Thirdly, as basically an economic agenda that facilitates faster, larger and more efficient flow of commodities and goods, and upgradation of production capacity, China's OBOR was not devised to be in a form of alliance, and does not require an elite membership. In other words, OBOR is very much like a public commodity with open access to all members of the world community, either as users or investors. If you feel you can benefit from it, take it. If you feel it's ugly and useless, maybe we can sit together to discuss how to improve it to suits your taste. This is a constructive way to go by. However, there is also a non-constructive way to resort to, for instance, to strongly discourage your friends from buying it, especially when they are really in need of it.

Fourthly, please understand, OBOR was an out of box proposal in the first place, when President Xi Jinping stepped into power in 2013. It's not perfect in the very beginning. Although it was welcomed by many states due to their great demand for connectivity, infrastructures, and production, there's always a lot of space for adjustment and improvement to ensure peace, stability and prosperity. But it would be too much of a request to ask China to convene an assembly of over 60 states to strive for a consensus on some particular demands of individual states. For the time being, I reckon, no country on the surface of this earth is capable of the job, not even the most powerful United States.

Most importantly, China is not ready to provide a ground for one state to judge or interfere with development plans of a third party, and regards this as respect that all sovereign states deserve. So as an essentially open initiative, OBOR does need consultation during its entire process with the participating states, as well as the potential participating states, but mostly on bilateral basis. This is exactly why we should reject the dispute about unilateralism and multilateralism over OBOR. Let's simply shift to bilateralism for a bit, because it is indeed the fair and proper description of Beijing's approach.

Consultation at Regional Level

It was suggested that *contemporary problems can be better solved at the regional rather than the bilateral or global levels*, (Mylonas & Yorulmazlar), and the concept of regional integration has been put in practice for more than two decades around the globe. In the case of SAARC, the natural bond at the economic and political front between the member states should undoubtedly be calculated into their individual development aspirations, as long as it does not put any of them in an awkward situation. It's becoming clearer that some countries in India's neighborhood take China's infrastructure and connectivity projects positively, because OBOR's promotion of policy coordination, facilities connectivity, unimpeded trade, financial integration and people-to-people bonds is not centered on any particular country.

Hamid Karzai stressed the need for a coordinated approach between India's Connect Central Asia Policy and China's OBOR initiative. A "positive symmetry" is needed between the two Asian neighbors. Chandrika Kumaratunga said India has the right to raise questions on the U.S. sale of fighter jets to Pakistan, Islamabad's sale of JF-17 aircraft to Sri Lanka, or the presence of Chinese submarines at Colombo or Male port. But India should not obstruct development projects supported by China in the region.

It is necessary to note that China has no intention to encourage or support any activities that build up tensions and disagreements within the subcontinent. Disagreement over trans-regional cooperation for infrastructural, economic and social development should not be the cause for antagonism. On the contrary, the Chinese Government encourages the countries along the Belt and Road to achieve economic policy coordination and carry out broader and more in-depth regional cooperation at higher level. To achieve this goal, consultations over connectivity agenda between the SAARC members seem to be advisable. It's even better if China can be invited to participate in this process.

Considering Secretary Jaishankar's preference for the consultation to be from "the conception stage itself", and our recognition and respect to India's dominant and leading role in South Asia, the India Government will be in the perfect position to advance such a dialogue for coordination at regional level, unless it has entirely dropped OBOR as an option.

Geopolitical Interpretation

The geopolitical reading into OBOR has been too much to be noteworthy. On many occasions, it was repeatedly publicized that hidden agendas could come in the way of its connectivity projects. An Indian Scholar from this institution was pretty right to say that usually war came with trade in history in his analysis of OBOR, to the extent that both China and India have fallen victims to the trade proposals of Western colonizers. Taking the peaceful expansion of China's economic footprints around the world for the past thirty seven years, however, this empirical argument can hardly sustain in the context of OBOR, which is in fact the 2nd version of China's economic expansion.

I am not very sure that I've followed the saying about hidden agendas aforementioned in its correct sense, but I understand well enough about the nexus between an overwhelming economic strength and its potential strategic consequences. Years back, the supervisor of my postdoc research once said to me, when we happened to touch upon the topic of China-US relations, that people tend to have a natural distaste for mammoth states. To ensure endurable peace and stability of this world, both China and the United States should be dismantled into small pieces. In one way or another, he could be right, because even small moves of major powers can make significant changes at the regional and global level, which may go way beyond the comfort scale of other states.

No matter how hard it tried, China is simply incapable of preventing India from raising geopolitical concerns over OBOR, for four reasons. Firstly, this is a mammoth initiative proposed by a mammoth state. Secondly, low level integration of South Asia due to the long-standing inter-state tensions guarantees division of stances over OBOR, which in turn would add up to the uncertainty in regional security dynamics. Thirdly, OBOR, that facilitates China's economic growth together with the countries along the route, could possibly get India's schedule to eliminate the structural inequality between the two delayed. Fourthly, a variety of sensitive issues, such as border dispute, squabble over trans-boundary water resource, trade deficit, Tibet issue, and China-India-Pakistan trilateral relations, though mostly kept under control, haunts us badly from time to time.

I kind of comprehended how big a difference that the geopolitical interpretation of OBOR can make, when taking a second look at what Prime Minister Modi said, loud and clear in the press statement in 2014, that *if* the two countries achieved "a climate of mutual trust and confidence, respect for each other's sensitivities and concerns, and, peace and stability in our relations and along our borders", *then* "we can reinforce each other's economic growth."

Three Years of OBOR

I'd like to take some time to share with you some statistics concerning OBOR since its launch three years ago.

The overall investment of China in the states along OBOR amounts to 51.1 billion US dollars, accounting for 12 per cent of its overseas investment. Chinese enterprises have won over 12 thousand construction contracts in the states along OBOR, with the total contract value standing at279 billion US dollars. Growth of investment to ASEAN and Central Asia was the highest in comparison with other regions along OBOR.

For a long term initiative, what Chinese enterprises achieved in the past three years has exceeded our expectation. Generally speaking, large companies are doing better than the small and medium-sized companies. With maturity in management, ample experiences in offshore business, and sound risk management system, Chinese multinationals, in their market exploration along OBOR, need less and less help from the central government. Therefore, focus of next stage will be on capability building of and financial support for small and medium sized companies in their OBOR adventure.

Conclusion

Having other South Asian states benefit from both the Chinese and Indian economies, by coordinating connectivity initiatives at regional and sub-regional level, such as road and rail connectivity in the BBIN, might not necessarily undermine India's leading role in the neighborhood, but can substantially relieve India of the pressure, financially and physically, to provide alternative options to its subcontinent partners.

Connectivity projects of OBOR, unfortunately failed the first round of the geopolitical test in India, are conceived to help states surpass the theater of geopolitics, and should not be given up that easily. If cooperation between China and India is still feasible, however, discussions on some innovative arrangements for certain projects on trilateral basis can be held, to ensure adequate involvement of India, transparent operation exclusively for civilian purpose, benefits sharing in proportion to contribution, etc.

It takes time, consultation, deliberation, patience and compromise for China to persuade India to join hands on OBOR. Let's pray it just won't take forever.

Perspectives on other Emerging Economic, Infrastructure and Trade Corridors in the Indo-Pacific

---

Ambassador Sanjay Singh, IFS (Retd)

I am delighted to join you in the second session of the USI seminar on the Indo-Pacific to share my 'Perspectives on other Emerging Economic, Infrastructure and Trade Corridors in the Indo-Pacific'.

This subject is vast and I intend to focus on the Indian perspective on both the soft and hard infrastructure taking shape in the region, the emerging trade regimes, the changing financial infrastructure, the utilization of global commons, the transport infrastructure based on road, rail, water-ways, sea and air, the energy grids built by oil and gas pipelines and power lines, the telecommunication network and digital connectivity.

At the outset, it bears emphasising that connectivity is key to socio-economic development, and all that this implies: improvement in the quality of life of people of people in the region, greater people-to-people exchanges, stimulating trade and investments. Connectivity includes not just physical connectivity but also institutional, regulatory, legal, digital, financial and commercial connectivity.

While developing connectivity and the economic, infrastructure and trade corridors in the Indo-Pacific we should aim to create arrangements which enhance trust and confidence. This can only be done if regional interactions are underpinned by commonly agreed international norms, rules and practices and respect for the global commons. India believes that it is important that we build our connectivity through a consultative process and not through unilateral decisions.

The Asian revival has ushered in a period of ever increasing change, when resurgent economies are creating new geo-economic and strategic paradigms. The emergence of India as an economic power is increasingly impacting developments in the Indo-Pacific region, a region which has benefited significantly from the forces of globalization and the consequent compression of geographic spaces.

This region is home to over 3.5 billion people with a combined Gross Domestic Product of over $ 20 trillion. It contains three of the world's four largest economies, - China, Japan and India. Growing economic interactions between the countries of the region are leading to the creation of new infrastructure and trade corridors as well as mechanisms towards addressing common challenges and creating a regional architecture to promote economic growth and prosperity.

Growing trade and investment between countries in the Indo-Pacific region generate demand for greater connectivity as well as the revival and upgradation of historical trade routes. As connectivity improves, a virtuous circle emerges by way of multiplier effects on national economies, new infrastructure and trade corridors.

It has been India's policy to focus on improving its infrastructure both within the country and with its neighbours. Thus there has been great attention paid to both the hard and soft infrastructure of road, rail, waterway and power networks both within and with our neighbours - Bhutan, Bangladesh, Nepal and Myanmar. However, bound as it is, by the Himalayas to the North and an inimical Pakistan to the North-West, India has given special attention to maritime linkages to enhance its connectivity with the rest of the world.

India's "Look East" policy, initiated in the 1990s spurred by our economic reforms, set India on the path of greater engagement with the world with a new emphasis on trade and the ocean surrounding us. India encompassed by the ocean on three sides has a coastline of 7500 km, 1200 islands and 2.4 million square kmof EEZ. Today, 90 percent of India's trade by volume and 90 percent of our oil imports are carried on the seas.

From the geo-strategic perspective, India sits atop strategic trade routes passing through the Indian Ocean linking West with East Asia as the fulcrum of a region spreading from the Eastern shores of Africa in the

West, the Bab-al–Mandab and the Straits of Hormuz through the Malacca and the South China Sea to Australia and the Western Pacific in the East.

Given all these factors, the importance of maritime trade for its own as well as global economic growth, it is but natural that India supports freedom of navigation and over flight, and unimpeded commerce through international waters, in keeping with the principles of international law and UNCLOS.

With almost 100,000 ships transiting through it annually, the Indian Ocean has the highest tonnage of goods traversing it of which more than 60,000 vessels transit through the Malacca straits. Over 10 million barrels of oil to Japan, South Korea, China, and other Pacific Rim countries passes through these straits every day. Dense and vital arteries of sea-borne energy and trade crisscross through the Indian Ocean.

The growing importance of the Indian Ocean to the global economy also provides greater salience to the Indian Ocean Rim Association (IORA) of which India is a founder member and ardent supporter. The IORA tries to identify opportunities for enhancing regional connectivity, economic cooperation and to develop shared interests.

India is also engaged in re-establishing the historic connectivities that existed around the Indian Ocean which it believes will be mutually beneficial. Project Mausam, whose name comes from the wind systems in the Indian Ocean is an initiative in this direction. It is a multi-disciplinary trans-national project that tries to rekindle long lost ties across the Indian Ocean Littoral and forge new avenues of cooperation and exchange between India and states of the Indian Ocean.

Similarly, at the initiative of the State Government of Kerala, supported by the Government of India there is an ongoing effort to revive the two millennia old "Spice Route".

A concerted move is also underway to revive the 'Cotton route' that linked seaports of the Indian Ocean Rim (IOR) to India a 1,000 years ago.

Essentially, these initiatives aim to support the economic growth of the Indo-Pacific region through creating new connectivities and economic corridors building on historical ties and precedents, but powered today by the economic forces driving the Asian revival.

Today, India has emerged as the third largest economy in Asia, a two trillion dollars plus economy that has joined the ranks of the top ten economies of the world. India represents a large and growing market for goods and services, an attractive destination for investment as well as a growing source of foreign investment and a cost effective hub for manufacturing, services and research & development. Digital connectivity is an essential component of India's connectivity with the region. India is connected to the Gulf, Africa and the West by undersea cables from Mumbai and Cochin. To the East it is connected from Trivandrum, Tuticorin, and Chennai. With the advances it has made in its space programme, India is an active player in setting up space based communication systems which provide connectivity within the region.

India has historically had close ties with countries of African littoral which were re-invigorated through the launch of Africa-India Forum Summit in 2008 in New Delhi. India-Africa trade has grown from around US $ 1 billion in 1991 to over US $ 66 billion in 2015-16 and there is robustly growing Indian investment in the region.

India has multi-faceted and mutually beneficial relations with the countries of West Asia. The Gulf is India's largest economic partner with trade of over $125 bn. in 2015-16. It provides energy security for India and over 8 million Indians reside in this region, constituting a significant source of investment and remittances. The combination of economic, human and energy connectivity creates immense synergies. Nearly 60 percent of our air traffic is to West Asia and Africa. India is a net security provider to the sea-borne energy exports of the Gulf region which traverse the sea-lanes around India.

Our economic ties today with each of our ASEAN (Association of Southeast Asian Nations) neighbours are multifaceted marked by growing trade and investment partnership. The Comprehensive Economic Cooperation Agreement (CECA) with Singapore was followed by another with Malaysia, an early harvest arrangement with Thailand and finally a Free Trade Agreement (FTA) with ASEAN as a whole. Our trade with ASEAN countries is over $70bn and there is an active investment relationship. India has also earmarked a special purpose vehicle to facilitate project financing and quick implementation and committed a Line of Credit of 1.0 billion U.S. dollars to promote projects that support physical and digital connectivity between India and ASEAN. A new thrust is being given to connectivity with South East Asia through the Kaladan multi-modal transport project that links Sittwe port in Myanmar to North-East India and the completion of the India- Myanmar- Thailand trilateral highway with extensions to Laos, Vietnam and Cambodia. Progress made in engagement with ASEAN is also reflected in India's participation in ASEAN-centric forums like the ASEAN Regional Forum (ARF), East Asia Summit (EAS)and India's intent to enhance connectivity with ASEAN countries and support the ASEAN Master-Plan-on-ASEAN-Connectivity-2025. Today, over 30 percent of Indian trade traverses the South China sea and 30 percent of Indian air traffic is towards the East.

Beyond ASEAN India has concluded Comprehensive Economic Partnership Agreement (CEPA) with both Japan and Korea and is in negotiations with Australia and New Zealand. India's trade with China has dramatically expanded. This is reflected in India's active participation in Asia–Europe Meeting (ASEM) and desire to engage with the Asia-Pacific Economic Cooperation (APEC) process. India is today fully engaged in the negotiations towards the creation of a regional trade block the RCEP (Regional Comprehensive Economic Partnership) and looks with interest at Trans-Pacific Partnership (TPP). India actively supports the activities of the World Bank and the Asian Development Bank and is an active participant in the new Asian Infrastructure Investment Bank (AIIB) and the BRICS New Development Bank with a view to support cross-border investments and infrastructure creation. India has also entered into currency swap arrangements with countries of the region to enhance financial stability.

India is itself in the process of transforming itself to becoming a part of regional value chains through programmes such as 'Make in India', 'Digital India ', 'Start up India' etc. There is also a new focus on port modernisation and port-led industrial development under the Sagarmala programme, which, when completed, willlead to a five-fold expansion of coastal shipping, transform inland waterways and create the maritime logistics required by a rapidly growing India and transform its 7500 km coastline and some of its islands into important enablers in national growth as well as growth of the Indo-Pacific. **The developments on the coast are accompanied by** road and rail development projects aimed at improving internal logistical efficiency and creation of internal economic corridors linked to regional corridors such as the Delhi-Mumbai Industrial Corridor and the Mumbai- Bengaluru- Chennai corridor. The latter is expected to connect to the Mekong-Dawei initiative. Studies are also underway on the Bangladesh-China-India-Myanmar BCIM corridor.

Within South Asia itself, connectivity can and does impart new economic momentum to the region. Some of it is happening through SAARC mechanisms, or through sub-regional arrangements as well as through bilateral or trilateral arrangements such as the CECA with Sri Lanka. In the BBIN (Bangladesh, Bhutan, India, Nepal) sub-region an ambitious agenda of rail and road connectivity, inland waterways, coastal shipping and energy cooperation is being implemented in addition to the free trade arrangements already in place.

Today a new emphasis is being given to coastal shipping along the littorals of the Bay of Bengal from Singapore to Sri Lanka in keeping with the desires of the participating countries in BIMSTEC (Bay of Bengal Initiative for Multi-sectoral technical and Economic Cooperation).Through our vision of "SAGAR" or Security and Growth for All in the Region, India is assisting in enhancing maritime logistics in Sri Lanka, Maldives, Mauritius and Seychelles and its littoral neighbours to fully develop the Blue Economy, build infrastructure to create onward connectivity from India. A Special Purpose Vehicle has been established to take up maritime projects overseas.

India's membership of the SCO (Shanghai Cooperation Organisation) has given a new impetus to our connectivity with Central Asia and building strong trade, transport, energy, digital and people to people links. India's decision to participate in the International North South Transport Corridor, join the Ashgabat Agreement and the Chabahar Agreement, reflects this desire and intent. India is also a member of the ambitious IPI (Iran, Pakistan, and India) and TAPI (Turkmenistan, Afghanistan, Pakistan, India) pipeline projects expected to supply gas from Iran and Turkmenistan to South Asia.

India, Iran and Russia agreed in September 2000 to develop the International North-South Transport Corridor (INSTC), a multi modal transport route from the Persian Gulf and the Indian Ocean through Iran and Russia and the Caspian Sea to Eurasia and to Europe viz.(Mumbai (India) to Bandar Abbas (Iran) by sea, from Bandar Abbas to Bandar-e-Anzali (an Iranian port on the Caspian Sea) by road/rail, and then from

Bandar-e-Anzali to Astrakhan (a Caspian port in the Russian Federation) by ship across the Caspian Sea, and thereafter from Astrakhan to other regions of the Russian Federation and further into Europe by Russian railways.

The INSTC was has expanded to include eleven new members, namely: Azerbaijan, Armenia, Kazakhstan, Kyrgyz Republic, Tajikistan, Turkey, Ukraine, Belarus, Oman, Syria, and Bulgaria (Observer). The completion of Turkmen-Kazakh section of the North South Railway line in May 2013 provides an alternate to the main INSTC route for connecting to Kazakhstan and beyond from the Iranian port of Bandar Abbas. Besides Bandar Abbas, this route can also be used from the Chabahar Port linking South Asia with Europe. Over time, we could even look to connect it with the sea and land based routes that India has developed with the Indian Ocean Region and South East Asia. This is expected to provide an impetus to connectivity and economic integration of the countries in the Eurasian region with those in the Indian Ocean and Persian Gulf.

India is also to join the Ashgabat Agreement that facilitates connectivity between the Indian Ocean and Central Asia. The Ashgabat Agreement has Oman, Iran, Turkmenistan, Uzbekistan and Kazakhstan as its members. Accession to this Agreement enables India to utilise the existing transport and transit corridor to facilitate trade and commercial interactions with the Eurasian region.

The Indian participation in the Chabahar port project in Iran and the trilateral agreement that Afghanistan, Iran and India have signed provides Afghanistan easy access to the sea and India better connectivity to Afghanistan and Central Asia. In May 2016, India entered into an arrangement with Iran that gives India the right to develop two berths of the Chabahar port and allows them to be operated for 10 years by India Ports Global. The trilateral transit agreement with Iran and Afghanistan links ports in the western coast of India to the Chabahar port and covers the road and rail links between Chabahar and the Afghan border. The corridor would spur unhindered flow of commerce throughout the region and lead to the development of gas based fertilizer plants and petrochemicals industry in Chabahar itself. Afghanistan will get an assured route to trade with the rest of the world. And for India it would provide connectivity to Afghanistan and the Central Asian countries.

In conclusion, it is worth pointing out that these projects are in various stages of progress and development. What is important is the political will and environment in all the countries concerned, to implement these projects. Both the political and economic climate need to be in concert in order for all these connectivities and infrastructure to achieve completion. India is playing a key role in the process and will continue to do so in co-operation with its partners in the various projects outlined above.

Blue Economy and Coastal Management in the Coming Decade

Admiral Dr. Jayanath Colombage

> *"Protecting our oceans is not a luxury. It is a necessity that contributes to our economy, our climate and our way of life. Working together, we can change the current course and chart a sustainable future"*
>
> – US Secretary of State John Kerry (2014)

The Ocean and Blue Economy

The ocean covers 71 percent of earth's surface and contains 97 percent of planet's water. This ocean is the life support system for the planet earth. The oceans have been playing a key role in the world for spreading civilizations, cultures, religions and affect the climate and weather. Humankind has been using the oceans since time immemorial for venturing for explorations, navigation, wars, trade, and leisure and for obtaining living and non-living resources. Oceans have been the main protein supplier for the humankind. With the gradual increase of population and depletion of land-based resources, many countries are now focusing even more attention on the oceans. The oceans have been the lifeline of many countries and the economic livewire as well. "Oceans carry 90 percent of internationally traded goods" (Spalding, 2010. p.3). Oceans generate half of the oxygen we breath (NOAA,2014).

Urbanization, pollution, over-exploitation and climate change can be detrimental to the sustenance of a balanced coastal ecosystem. There is a growing awareness in the world today that we need to be careful about exploiting the ocean based economy, as we cannot afford to damage the very ocean that is our lifeline. This new area of focus is termed as 'Blue

Economy'. Blue Economy refers to a sustainable ocean based economic model that is largely dependent on coastal and marine ecosystems and resources. It is one that employs environmentally sound and innovative infrastructure, technologies and practices including institutional and financing arrangements for meeting goals of:

a. Sustainable and inclusive development;

b. Protecting our coasts and oceans, and reducing environmental risks and ecological scarcities;

c. Addressing water, energy and food security;

d. Protecting the health, livelihoods and welfare of the people in the coastal zone;

e. Fostering an ecosystem-based climate change mitigating and adaptation measures.

(Ebarvia, 2016. p.3)

There is renewed understanding about the oceans as a key natural source for national as well as regional economies. This understanding has led to increased concern about ecological health and sustainability of oceans. This has compelled number of states to take measures to study the economic value of the oceans and to take measures to protect them (Colgan,2016). It is not always possible to measure the economic value of oceans and ocean based resources. Colgan explains this further "however, unlike many other natural resource based industries, the oceans' complex mixture of extractive resources, its influence on the land in the coastal regions, and the diversity of geographic circumstances ranging from islands to continents make the measure of economic value a particularly challenging proposition" (2016. p.2). Unless the world understands the economic value and is able to quantify, it will be difficult to convince governments and other agencies involved in ocean based economic activities, the need to safeguard and protect the oceans and use them in a sustainable manner.

In order to derive sustainable results, the linkage between the Blue economy, economic growth and ocean and coastal resource conservation need to be properly understood. As Ebarvia points out "The blue economy encompasses all economic activities with a direct dependence on the ocean or coastal marine sources" (2016. p.3). These activities can be categorized as ocean-based and ocean-related. Ocean-based activities are those undertaken in the ocean such as fisheries and aquaculture, offshore oil and gas, mining, ocean energy, desalination, shipping/marine transportation, marine tourism and construction. "The ocean-related activities are the ones, which uses products from the ocean, such as seafood processing, marine biotechnology, chemicals, salt and other products and services for ocean and ocean-based activities such as shipbuilding and repair, ports, tourist resorts, communication, marine insurance and law, and marine technical services" (Ebarvia, 2016. p.3). Another key area of Blue Economy is marine research and education involving public as well as private agencies such as navies, coast guards, marine environment protection agencies and academic institutes. However, it must be understood that some of the economic values generated by the oceans cannot be quantified, such as habitats for fish and other marine life, carbon sequestration, shoreline protection, waste recycling and storing and the influence on climate and biodiversity. There are some new activities evolving in recent years such as desalination, marine biotechnologies, ocean energy, and seabed mining as well. These new activities too have an impact on the Blue Economy.

Threats to Blue Economy

Offshore Oil and Gas. There are many risks associated with oil and gas exploration and related extraction processes. There can be accidental oil spills and release of gas at sea during storage and shipping. Harbours and terminals facilitating storage and loading of oil and gas have the threat of accidental release. This could harm human life, wildlife and coastal regions.

Commercial and Recreational Fishing. Overfishing for global seafood trade is a major threat to the sustenance of the oceans. Illegal, Unreported and Unregulated (IUU) fishing is taking place in world's oceans, despite various international and regional conventions and regimes. Some fisheries also employ destructive fishing methods such as bottom trawling, use of explosives, banned nets. etc. These methods are harmful to the reproduction cycle of various species of fish,their habitats and can destroy an entire marine eco-system. Also there are large numbers of recreational fishing activities taking place in the oceans. The biggest source of protein to the mankind is at huge risk from over exploitation and destruction.

Aquaculture Projects. Aquaculture production meets more than half the global seafood need now (Spalding, 2016.p.7). Presently much of the production is land based. However, there is a possibility for this business to venture in to the coastal areas. This could result in habitat destruction, pollution by use of chemicals, discharge of nutrients, microbial pathogens, drugs, herbicides and fungicides (Spalding, 2016). Even from land based aquaculture projects, the possibility is there for these pollutants to enter the ocean through streams or with rainwater. This can have an adverse impact on the fisheries in coastal regions.

Shipping. Shipping is considered as the most 'carbon efficient' means of transportation of goods. The situation has further improved with Triple E class (Economy of scale, Energy efficient and Environment friendly) mega container vessels coming in to operation. However, shipping is still a substantial emitter of greenhouse gases, acoustic pollution, oil spills and other types of pollution. As per Spalding "International Maritime Organization (IMO) estimates that CO2 emissions from shipping are about 3 percent of the global human caused emissions and expect to continue to rise to meet the demand for international trade" (2010, p.8). Shipbreaking can be a dangerous industry unless properly regulated and safety standards are scrupulously met. There can be many toxic materials, which had been used in ship construction, especially in old ships, such as asbestos. Asbestos fiber can enter human respiratory track through inhalation causing cancer. Ships are coated with tons of paint containing lead, cadmium, organotin, arsenic, zinc and chromium. There also can be various sealants used in PCBs (Hossain and Islam, 2012). These are considered as hazardous waste and remain intact in the environment for long periods. These could be distributed widely and can enter the humans and other mammals, fish and other animals through the food chain. This can pose a severe threat to the human population, wild life and coastal environment.

Ships also contain large quantities of residual oils and lubricants. These can be spilled and mix with the seawater and left floating along the seashore. These spills can reduce the light intensity beneath the water, which inhibit photosynthesis, restrict exchange of oxygen and carbon dioxide, which can be harmful to aquatic life and cause damage to bird population by coating their feathers and causes buoyancy and insulation losses (Hossain and Islam, 2012). Shipbreaking can lead to severe labour abuses and minimal environmental mitigation. This activity can pollute beaches and coastal waters and has human security implications, especially to coastal communities.

Coastal Tourism. Coastal tourism is a major industry in many of the coastal countries. There can be unsustainable and disruptive tourist activities taking place in these areas. Spalding says "many coastal regions around the world are under siege from impact of inappropriate tourism development" (2010, p.8). Unauthorized construction of infrastructure, discharge of untreated sewage and some other coastal tourist activities can also lead to coastal erosion, depleting of mangroves plantations and seriously threaten local wildlife and their habitats. This can affect the livelihood of coastal population and also one of the main attractions that tourists come for.

Telecommunications. "Submarine cables carry 95 percent of all global telecommunications, connecting 2.7 billion users and supporting global business, finance and entertainment, etc." (Cicn-sain, 2015).These cable can however, interfere with the benthic zone of the seabed and cause harm to the seabed.

New Industries in Blue Economy

Renewable Energy. The ocean offers various types of renewable energy including wind, wave, tidal, current, and Ocean Thermal Energy Conversion (OTEC). This renewable energy can be an alternative for fossil fuel sourced energy. By obtaining renewable energy from the ocean near to the markets, the long distance transmission cost and loss can be minimized. However, some of the technologies such as offshore wind farms, carbon sequestration: tidal and wave energy: and OTEC can be threatening to coastal marine ecosystem.

Seabed Mining. As the natural resources on land is rapidly depleting due to increasing world population and over exploitation, it is quite natural that the humankind look for exploitation of the seabed for obtaining raw materials. As the oceans are vast there is a perception that seabed resources may be unlimited. This could present the oceans with an enormous threat, including damaging seabed biomass and polluting water column, which could harm the balance of marine ecosystem. Activities aimed at harnessing the finite seabed resources, which could do irreversible damage to the ecosystem should be carefully considered and the impact should be minimized as much as possible.

Remediation/restoration. Remediation is restoring the ecosystem. Humans can restore what they destroy. Design, construction, operation, and monitoring of large -scale coastal and marine restoration projects can create jobs and help to restore the ecosystem, which will support coastal livelihoods.

Blue Biotechnology. This is extraction of marine species for use for biotechnology. As Ebarvia points out "The ocean is now considered as the last frontier in the search for novel drugs from nature to serious human diseases such as cancer, AIDS, tuberculosis and drug resistant infections" (2016). It is believed that some lifesaving medicines can be found from the deep ocean. Unless this process is well coordinated and regulated, the competition to extract these species could harm the eco system in the long run.

Blue Technology. This sector includes providing of infrastructure, sensors, instruments and platforms to manage and communicate ocean data, software tools and models, marine robotics, and environmental safety and compliance technology companies. These can help to conserve the ecosystem without being allowing for over exploitation.

Coastal Management: The Way Forward

There is no doubt that the Blue Economy is the way forward for the humankind in the next decades to come. The humankind has no alternative but to use the blue economic activities to sustain and prosper. However, it must be understood that even the vast oceans contain finite resources only and any exploitation or extraction has to be done keeping this in mind. Even renewable energy needs time to recover. Unless the world exploits the oceans in the sustainable manner, the worst affected will be the coastal communities. The livelihood of this community depends heavily on the resources they harvest from the oceans. In order to understand the way forward in coastal management, the Goal 14 of the United Nations resolution 70/1, "Transforming our world: The 2030 Agenda for Sustainable Development" will be used. The main objective of Goal 14 of this agenda, 'Life Below Water' is to "conserve and sustainably use oceans, seas and marine resources for sustainable development" (UN, 2015). The main thrust of this is to involve both citizens and exploiters in the Blue Economy, to shift subsidies away from environmentally harmful activities to promote pursuits that enhance public goods and ocean resources, sustainable marine economic activities that meet the needs of current and future generation and to create ocean foundations to foster and formulate the new Blue Economy. The objectives for management of the coast and near coast waters as per the targets of Goal 14 are as follows:

1. Prevention and significantly reducing all kinds of marine pollution from all platforms at sea and specially from land-based activities including marine debris and nutrient pollution. There is a need to manage ballast water and invasive species management from ships.

2. Sustainably manage and protect marine and coastal ecosystems to avoid significant adverse impacts. Take actions for restoration of the coastal areas and vegetation including mangroves in order to achieve healthy and productive oceans

3. Minimize and address the impact of ocean acidification, including through enhanced scientific cooperation at all levels. Minimize dumping of industrial waste and other form of discharges to the ocean.

4. Effectively regulate harvesting and overfishing, IIU fishing and destructive fishing practices and implement science-based management plans. Restore fish stocks to a level which can produce maximum sustainable yield. Ban selling of IUU fishing and compel markets not to sell those IUU products.

5. Conservation of at least a certain percentage of coastal and marine areas, consistent with national and international law and based on available scientific information. Prohibit use of certain coastal areas and declare them as conservation sites.

6. Increase economic benefits to small island developing states and least developed countries from the sustainable use of marine resources, including through sustainable management of fisheries, aquaculture and tourism.

7. Increases scientific knowledge, develop research capacity and transfer marine technology, in order to improve ocean and coastal health and to enhance contribution of marine biodiversity to the development of developing countries. Enhance the conservation and sustainable use of oceans and their resources by implementing international law as reflected in UNCLOS, which provides legal framework for the conservation and sustainable use of oceans and their resources.(UN, 2015)

There is a requirement to develop partnerships by all stakeholders related to the ocean and coastal areas to preserve the very ocean, where the future of the humankind lies. These stakeholders could include governmental and non-governmental organizations, financial institutes, scientific community, civil society organization, academic institutes and international agencies such as UN or regional associations. It is necessary to share experiences of each other in conserving the planet's oceans and the coastal systems for the sake of future of humankind.

Conclusion

There is no doubt that the oceans are the lifelines of humankind. Many countries are now looking to the oceans to obtain resources. Although the oceans are vast, humankind should not attempt to extract/exploit ocean based resources in a manner harmful to the ecosystem. The Blue Economy refers to a sustainable ocean based economic model that is largely dependent on coastal and marine ecosystem and resources. It calls for environmentally sound and innovative infrastructure, technologies and practices including institutional and financial arrangements for meeting goals of the Blue Economy. It is not always possible to quantify the economic value of the ocean based resources. The Blue Economy encompasses all economic activities with a direct dependence on the coastal or coastal marine sources.

Threats to Blue Economy can come from various activities such as oil and gas industry, commercial and recreational fishing including IUU and destructive fishing, shipping and associated discharging of harmful materials, coastal tourism, telecommunication projects and some other ocean based economic activities. There is a need for concentrated efforts by all stakeholders including the public to minimize these threats. There are some new industries coming up in the Blue Economy such as obtaining renewable energy, seabed mining, remediation/restoration the ecosystem, Blue biotechnology, Blue technology, which includes sensors, instruments, robotics, environmental safety and compliance technology companies, which could help to conserve the ecosystem whilst allowing for sustainable harvesting.

The United Nations has come up with a positive and milestone based agenda in 2015 called 'transforming our world: the 2030 agenda for sustainable development'. The main thrust of this agenda is to "conserve and sustainably use oceans, seas and marine resources for sustainable development". The coastal management in the coming decade should be undertaken based on this goal, as it encompasses the entire world for sustainable development. There is a need for careful planning of coastal and sea areas, and management of ecosystems. There is also a need to understand the ocean and ocean based resources in a scientific manner and this could mitigate the possible negative consequences from Blue Economic activities and even external events such as storms, climate change, and environmental changes such as sea level rising. Blue Economy is our future and we need to act now and not after some valuable ocean resources are destroyed in the name of development.

Reference

Cicin-Seain,B. (2015). Goal14- Conserve and Sustainably use Oceans Seas and Marine Resources for Sustainable Development, *UN Chronicle, April 20005,* Available at:

http://unchronicle.un.org/article/goal-14-conserve-and-sustainably-use-oceans-seas-and-marine-resource-sustainable [Accessed : 20th Sep 2016]

Ebarvia, M.C. (2016). Economic Assessment of Oceans for Sustainable Blue Economy Development, *Journal of Oceans and Coastal Economics, Vol. 2, Article 7.* Available at: http://dx.doi.org/10.15351/2373-8456.1051 [Accessed: 19TH Sep 2016]

Colgan, C.S. (2016) Introduction to special Edition: The Oceans and National Income Accounts: An international Perspective. *Journal of Oceans and Coastal Economics, Vol. 2, Article1.*Available at: http://dx.doi.org/10.15351/2373-8456.1054 [Accessed: 19TH Sep 2016]

Hossain, M.M and Isalam, M.M (2012) Environmental Pollution: Ship Breaking in Bangladesh, *Young Power In Social Action (YPSA),* Available at: https://www.shipbreakingbd.info/Environment.html [Accessed: 3rd Oct 2016]

NOAA. (2014) Marine Organisms Produce half of the Oxygen that Land Animals need to Breathe, Available at: http://oceanexplorer.noaa.gov/facts/oceanproduction.html. [Acccssed: 20th Sep 2016]

Spalding, M.J.(2016) The New Blue Economy: The Future of Sustainability, *Journal of Oceans and Coastal Economics, Vol. 2, Article 8,* Available at: http://dx.doi.org/10.15351/2373-8456.1052 [Accessed: 19TH Sep 2016]

United Nations (2015) Sustainable Development Goals. Available at: https://sustainabledevelopment.un.org/sdg14 [Accessed: 23rd Sep 2016]

Challenges to Regional Economic Integration In Indian Ocean Region: Way Forward

Dr Mohammad Jasim Uddin

Indian Ocean Region

In general, the Indian Ocean Region (IOR) is "defined as including the Arab Gulf, East Africa, South Asia, East Asia to the Strait of Malacca, Southern Ocean, Asia and Australia"[1]. Indian Ocean Rim Association (IORA) is the only pan Indian Ocean (IO) "economic grouping and brings together 21 countries straddling three continents i.e. Africa, Asia and Australia"[2]. Study of Cordesman and Toukan divides IOR into 36 countries of five sub-regions: the Middle-east and Gulf, Red Sea and Horn, East Africa and Sub-Sahara, South Asia, and Southeast Asia/Oceania.[3] Central Intelligence Agency (CIA) *World Factbook* "estimates that IO covers 68.556 million sq km and includes the Andaman Sea, Arabian Sea, Bay of Bengal, Flores Sea, Great Australian Bight, Gulf of Aden, Gulf of Oman, Java Sea, Mozambique Channel, Persian Gulf, Red Sea, Suva Sea, Strait of Malacca, Timor Sea and other tributary water bodies"[4]. It has major ports in India, Sri Lanka, Indonesia, South Africa and Australia. All these aforesaid substantiate that defining IOR with areas and states is problematic. IOR states are different

1 Anthony H. Cordesman and Abdullah Toukan, *The Indian Ocean Region A Strategic Net Assessment*, New York: Centre for Strategic and International Studies (CSIS), August 2014, p. 2.

2 Vijay Sakhuja, "The Indian Ocean in 2015", *Institute of Peace and Conflict Studies (IPCS) Forecasts 2015*, Special Report No. 67, January 2015, p. 9.

3 Anthony H. Cordesman and Abdullah Toukan, *op. cit.*, p. ix.

4 *Ibid.*,p. 1.

regarding their economic growth and development level, politico-security scenario, socio-cultural status, etc. These make a diverse mix of prospect and also insecurity. IO is an important Sea Lines of Communication (SLOC) within the IOR and between the West and the East. It is the IOR through which a significant chunk of oil and petroleum is exported by the Gulf countries. Being a key international energy trading route, geo-economic and geo-strategic significance of the IOR is thus evident.

Regional Economic Integration

There are five stages of Regional Economic Integration (REI): Free Trade Area (FTA), Customs Union (CU), Common Market (CM), Economic Union (EU) and Complete Economic Integration (CEI). Some advocate one more step - Preferential Trading Agreement (PTA) before an FTA. In PTA, trade between members within the agreement apply comparatively lower tariffs than trade between members and non-members (i.e. outsiders). In FTA, trade-related all barriers are removed between/among members. Here also, members have freedom to trade with non-members, but with diverse trade policies. North American Free Trade Agreement (NAFTA) is an instance. A basic distinction between FTA and CU is that in the latter, members, besides removing all trade barriers between themselves, also agree to have trade with outsiders by a nearly similar approach. Gulf Cooperation Council (GCC) is an instance. Some key aspects of CM are (i) creation of markets integrated economically (ii) removal of all barriers to trade (iii) elimination of all constraints for labour and capital movement (iv) common trade policy for outsiders, etc. Common Market for Eastern and Southern Africa (COMESA) is an instance. Two vital aspects of EU are: (i) removal of all trade barriers and (ii) adoption of common economic policies, by signing an economic agreement, within a group of states. European Union is an instance. Monetary Union (MU), approval of common currency, fixed exchange rates between/among currencies, synchronisation of fiscal and monetary policies are some crucial aspects of CEI.

Some Existing Arrangements of REI in IOR

Littoral or coastal states of IOR and states that have and will have geo-political and geo-economic impacts by the IO have already formed several arrangements for REI.

Arrangements	Major Initiatives
IORA	Examining possibility of forming PTA
SAARC	Reducing products from sensitive list and continuing trade liberalisation programme to implement SAFTA, in a process of exchanging lists of offer and request and finalising schedules of commitments under SATIS.
BIMSTEC	Tariff Reduction Process (TRP) is in progress through fast and normal track approach to implement BIMSTEC FTA.
ASEAN	ASEAN+3 (JCK) = EAFTA, ASEAN+6 (JCK+ANZI) = RCEP, AFTA (including service sector and investment)+AFAS(ASEAN Framework Agreement on Services)+AIA(ASEAN Investment Area) = AEC, etc.
RCEP	Few decisions are undertaken - unification of supply chain networks, tariff elimination on a high percentage of tariff lines and trade value, cooperation in trade in goods and services, investment, competition, Intellectual Property (IP), economic and technical, dispute settlement, etc.
APTA	Signing agreements on trade facilitation, investment protection and liberalisation of trade in services, increasing percentage of tariff preferences on increasing number of items for LDCs, deepening of tariff concession, increase of product coverage e.g. Non-Tariff Barriers (NTBs).
TPP	An inter-regional FTA with high-level commitment in tariff elimination and in making new rules on trade, investment, IP Rights (IPRs), environmental protection, labour, Technical Barriers to Trade (TBT), etc.
APEC	Undertaking a study to realise FTAAP, launching ease of doing business action plan, streamlining customs procedures, endorsing APEC new strategy for structural reform to foster competition and better functioning markets.

Arrangements	Major Initiatives
D-8	Signing PTA, TRP in progress, working on value addition criterion of Rules of Origin (RoO).
GCC	Launching CM in 2008 to realise integrated single market, launching CU that was fully operational in 2015, undertaking steps to ensure creation of a single currency, launching common economic projects, etc.

Note: SAARC (South Asian Association for Regional Cooperation), SAFTA (South Asian Free Trade Area), SATIS (SAARC Agreement on Trade in Services), BIMSTEC (Bay of Bengal Initiative for Multi-Sectoral Technical and Economic Cooperation), ASEAN (Association of South East Asian Nations), JCK (Japan, China and Republic of Korea), EAFTA (East Asian Free Trade Area), ANZI (Australia, New Zealand and India), RCEP (Regional Comprehensive Economic Partnership), AFTA (ASEAN Free Trade Area), AEC (ASEAN Economic Community), APTA (Asia-Pacific Trade Agreement), LDCs (Least Developed Countries), TPP (Trans-Pacific Partnership), APEC (Asia-Pacific Economic Cooperation), FTAAP (Free Trade Area of the Asia-Pacific), D-8 (Developing Eight).

Source: Compiled from various documents.

Challenges to REI in IOR

Most of the arrangements in IOR are in very initial stage of REI. Economic Integration (EI) has been limited due to slow progress in trade facilitation and trade liberalisation programmes e.g. sluggishness in TRP, divergence on products in sensitive and negative lists, difference on value addition criteria of RoO, varied customs procedure, NTBs, Non Tariff Measures (NTMs), inadequate supply chain networks and lack of commitment to scheduled timeframe, etc. GCC and ASEAN are in some way exceptions. Though, fully operational CM and creation of single currency are in progress in GCC, and AFTA with re-scheduled timeframe for intra-ASEAN tariff elimination is seeing little progress on AFTA-plus items e.g. services, investment, NTBs, harmonisation of standards, etc.

Markets of IOR, particularly because of policy-oriented barriers, are fragmented not only in services but also in agriculture and manufacturing.

For regional consumption, little is regional production. A big chunk eyes markets in the West. Thus, rather weak is REI. Another concern is difference in openness between trade/Foreign Direct Investment (FDI) and finance. Trade/FDI-to-Gross Domestic Product (GDP) ratio is high in many states of East (e.g. China) and South-east Asia. Openness in trade or FDI is also ever-increasing in South Asia. But, financial openness is rather low in the regions. It is mainly owing to restrictive *policies governing openness* in finance in comparison with *those* in trade/FDI, particularly in manufacturing. Such protectionism decelerates regional integration more in finance, even than in trade.

There are concerns with FTAs. They are keen more on tariff cuts but less on NTBs. REI is more impeded by NTBs than tariff cuts. Hence, domestic firms, suppliers of services and agricultural products, Multinational Companies (MNCs) with their industrial Global Supply Chains (GSCs) and final consumers are affected. These are available in East Asia. Since, the region has given significant emphasis on lowering tariffs relatively. On the other hand, tariffs though are higher in nature in South Asia, but decreasing in gradual manner. What is important to state is that NTBs is high in South Asia, in fact highest in the world.

A crucial aspect of the FTAs is that they are burdened with conflicting RoO. The RoO is overloaded with dissimilar standards for varied products and creates different complexities. For sensitive imports, even in the same agreement, RoO is sometimes stringent and different. That creates dilemma for domestic producers. Things are very complicated between agreements. As an instance, FTAs between Japan and Malaysia and between Japan and Thailand have varying RoO in the case of automobiles. It reminds that "this is the *noodle-bowl*, the Asian equivalent of the global *spaghetti bowl* of overlapping FTAs with discriminatory provisions"[5]. Managing FTA stipulations, intricate schedules of tariff and fulfilling RoO increase production costs. Therefore, in the direction of trade liberalisation or trade facilitation, FTAs remain fragile. In turn, it impedes regional integration mechanism.

5 Razeen Sally, "Regional Economic Integration in Asia: The Track Record and Prospects", ECIPE Occasional Paper No. 2, 2010, p. 11.

Not so likely it is to anticipate that big-number-group collaboration would generate a mega regional FTA. That demands undertaking extraordinary policy measures in resolving broader divergences for a number of issues within several FTAs concluded at bilateral and plurilateral levels and in folding all to a mega trans-regional FTA. The issues are quantitative restrictions, tariff rates, Special and Differential (S&D) treatment, sector-oriented liberalisations, RoO and a number of different stipulations. If the issues are not convincingly settled, outcome would be again a trade-light FTA. This will really hamper to undertake reforms at national level and liberalisation unilaterally. This in turn will hinder REI in the IOR.

A vital issue is that integration in trade and investment has been market-oriented and bottom-up in East Asia. It is obvious while one looks at FTAs/groups e.g. AFTA/EAFTA. Importantly, unilateral trade-and-FDI liberalisation has helped promote regional integration. Such mechanism helped Japan, USA and several MNCs to form "vertically-integrated production networks, linked to GSCs and final markets in the West"[6]. East Asia accordingly observes *tilted* regional integration, with far-flung dreams of single market, monetary union or collaboration in finance. Institutions hardly play a vital role. Being the least mal-integrated one in the world, the case of South Asia in REI is seriously in question. To sum up, the practice of regionalism with fragile foundation(s) is inadequate and that is the challenge of REI in the IOR.

Besides, various alliances with diverse memberships, imprecise planning and politico-economic differences, limited dependency on existing arrangements, concerns between/among almost similar FTAs, conflict over maritime territory or marine resources and involvement of extra-regional powers are not only determining but also critical factors in the case of REI within the IOR.

6 *Ibid.*,p. 13.

Figure 1: ASEAN, RCEP and TPP

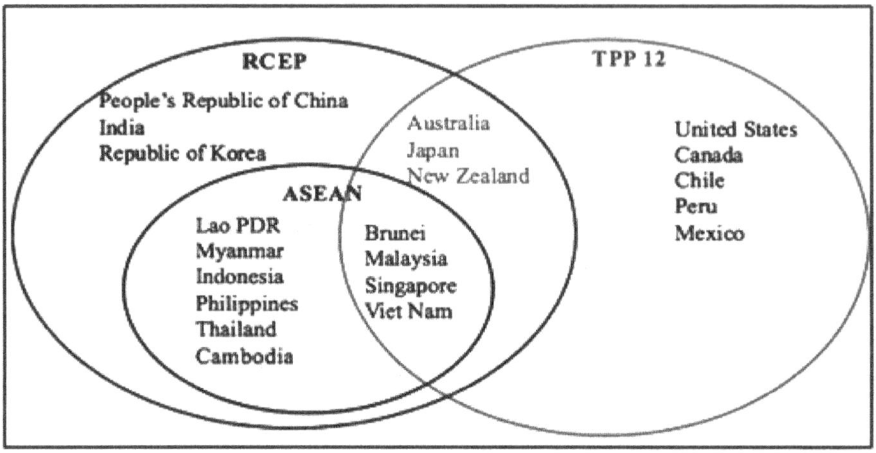

Table 1: RCEP vs. TPP: Comparisons, Characteristics and Concerns[7]

	RCEP	TPP
Comparisons	Led by ASEAN Born out of ASEAN+1 FTAs with JCK and ANZI Based on open accession clause, where membership can be expanded later as they sign FTA with ASEAN	Led by USA Born out of P4 agreement between New Zealand, Brunei, Singapore and Chile APEC countries are encouraged to join negotiations; also open to accession by non-APEC members

7 Available at https://www.brookings.edu/wp-content/uploads/2014/01/11-asia-pacific-economic-integration-presentation-basu-das.pdf, accessed on 10 October 2016.

Characteristics	To form an integrated regional economic agreement that is deeper than existing FTAs and support equitable economic development Areas - liberalise trade in goods, services and investment, technical cooperation, IP, dispute settlement (WTO+ issue)	To establish regional FTA to tackle challenges of 21st century Areas - liberalise trade in goods, services, investment, IPRs, environmental protection, labour, financial services, TBT and other regulatory issue (WTO+ issue)
Concerns	Building on *ASEAN Way* and differential treatment depending on level of members' development could contribute to slower progress Conflict due to tension between China and USA ASEAN+1 FTAs have different features and are at different stages of implementation	Gold standard 21st century FTA and addresses next generation issues (cross-cutting/new trade challenges) Does not include China and India May divide ASEAN as all are not participating in TPP and that may undermine ASEAN's centrality

Note: WTO (World Trade Organization)

There is a question whether TPP and RCEP would earn benefit or curse for ASEAN (see Figure 1 and Table 1). Academics are divided whether the two would have competition as both are nearly similar pacts wishing for liberalising trade and EI. Some argue that TPP might be challenged by RCEP as the former requires deeper integration in a more number of areas than the latter. Based on areas focused by RCEP, critics argue that it would be "a partial WTO-plus deal". Nevertheless, both pacts give rise to antagonism with each other owing to the deeper involvement of China and the US. Since, both countries for securing their future business interests, there is desire to be deeply economically engaged with East and South-east Asian regions. Consequently, rivalry between the two might also be a critical factor in how economic architecture of the IOR develops.

In the IOR, multiple-level efforts (e.g. TTP, RCEP, FTAAP, etc.) to facilitate EI are in progress. With different dimensions, possibilities, groupings, stipulations and measures, the efforts or arrangements are different. Countries with different socio-economic backgrounds within ASEAN are party to the trade agreements. With multifaceted and sometimes overlapping policy initiatives, the agreements call for having mega economic blocs but at the same time they induce leadership competition in a region. Besides international facet, unilateral i.e. country-by-country position may affect negotiations, developments and finally accomplishments of the trade agreements.

Indo-pacific region or the IOR in broader sense is now a focus spot of international economy with regards to trade, marine resources and energy transportation over the Western as well as the Eastern Sea Lines of Communications (SLOCs) to the West, East and South Asia. Owing to the escalating criticality of the IOR for geo-strategic as well as geo-economic grounds (e.g. maritime connectivity, blue economy, contestation over maritime territories and marine resources), important global powers including energy traders have ever-increasing stakes in partnerships with the IOR nations. China's Belt and Road initiative, its attractive offers to the IO states and quest for supporting Maritime Silk Route (MSR), India's projects like Mausum, Spice Route and Sagar Mala are also symptomatic of how emerging and traditional powers are active in the IOR.

There are different geo-strategic stakes and interests of different powers (e.g. regional and extra-regional) in the IOR. The stakes and interests generate impacts at state and regional levels. Ensuring peace, development and stability on the one side and making partnerships on trade and investment opportunities as well as trading raw materials on the other are important stakes for both IOR states and extra-regional powers. In the IOR, amid the extra regional influences, the US is a key military power. It has a number of port access and basing agreements with several states of the IOR. In the security dynamics of the IO, a new entrant is the European Union. Also evident is the engagement of China and Japan.

Furthermore, "Russian navy's show of 'flag' and 'presence' in IO reflects its ambition to engage in distant water operations"[8].

From strategic and economic viewpoints, IO creates scope for maritime cooperation. But, the rise of naval affairs by several IOR states and the increasing extra regional influence give rise to competitive dynamics. Securitisation and stabilisation of IOR relies lot upon how IOR states' economic progress and energy importers beyond the region shape overall scenario in trade and FDI, and specifically the Gulf's energy export flow. On the other hand, divergences might prevail within South-east Asian states, amid which, concern on security with regard to China could be a source of splitting up over any mega trade bloc e.g. RCEP. Particularly, politico-security relationship is being deteriorated owing to anxieties between some nations of the region and China on the rise of disputes on South China Sea. This could interrupt joint endeavours of China and ASEAN i.e. broader economic integration.

To summarise, conflict over maritime territory, maritime connectivity and marine resources by emerging regional and extra regional powers will, in addition to trade and economic divergences, also remain as crucial challenge for REI in the IO region.

Way Forward

With multifaceted focus and multipronged agendas, the IOR has limitations with existing institutions that are yet to significantly facilitate its REI. Hence, some of existing arrangements must exclusively focus on economic issues. 'Bottom-up' approach might be a key to work EI. But, for that guiding principles and institutions must develop at least within leading members. A principle could be to renew and speed up unilateral trade and FDI liberalisation. This will help (i) MNC supply chains to spread out in services, manufacturing and agriculture, and (ii) regional markets to be really unlocked for domestic producers and consumers. Another policy could be to accelerate state-by-state autonomous liberalisation. It will help address both border and non-border barriers. In brief, existing arrangements must develop trade facilitation measures.

8 Available at http://www.ipcs.org/columnist/vijay-sakhuja/, accessed on 10 October 2016.

- Amid existing arrangements, ASEAN could lead to facilitate TPP and RCEP's co-existence. It will help examining a mega trade bloc i.e. FTAAP. That will have an opportunity to combine TPP's high-standard liberalisation, RCEP's S&D treatment and open accession. Critics argue that such mega-regional approach e.g. mega-FTAs might be unattainable. Since, inbuilt divergences within the approach may interrupt not only flourishing GSCs but also existing and future EI. With intra-IOR politico-economic concerns, it may end up as another trade-light pact. Some argue that RCEP might matter more to IOR. But for that following should be taken into consideration:

- Increasing negotiation power of South-east Asian nations in RCEP, developing ASEAN's institutional arrangements to integrate policies and measures amid its members, reducing disagreements on IPRs and being aware of RCEP's welfare effects on members of ASEAN.

- Gradually minimising interest-oriented divergences amid RCEP partners; being cautious about the flexibility clause in the pact; lessening discrepancies between or among prevailing FTAs; dealing carefully with NTBs in trade and investment and easing RoO criteria to better functionalise the FTAs; speeding up of RCEP's tariff elimination coverage and services liberalisation programmes.

Stimulating liberalisation in trade is very essential for the IOR for opening markets, advancing global value chains and furthering growth even in critical economic downturn. Besides trade and investment integration, the region must practice and implement financial integration. To mobilise resources, recently established Asian Infrastructure Investment Bank and New Development Bank, besides traditional global financial institutions, could be useful alternatives. Being aware of politico-security concerns and interests of extra regional powers is also vital as these could scratch IOR's REI initiatives. Even the IOR states need to fix and re-fix time to time their politico-economic priorities. However, REI of IOR depends lot on how far states of the region will be dedicated to the application of regional integration in the schemes of EI.

PART – III

Emerging Architecture in the Indo-Pacific Region: Way Forward

A Prognosis of Competing Economic Architecture in the Indo-Pacific Region (RCEP, TPP and other Economic Institutions): Way Forward

Ms Tsun-Tzu Hsu

Introduction

A number of mega Free Trade Agreements (FTAs) have emerged in the past years with potentials to constitute major trade architectures in the world. Among the initiatives, the Trans Pacific Partnership (TPP), already concluded and signed by its 12 original members, contains high quality liberalization and regulatory provisions in a number of chapters which, if entry into force, will change the existing regional value chains and rules making of trade and economic activities in the region. However, if the TPP fails to be ratified, the RCEP will be of emerging importance and then the Indo Pacific region and India should play a more active role in promoting a 'rebalancing" of economic integration to focus more on improvement of human skills and physical infrastructure. Thus, the Make in India can be a new model in bringing economic growth and create job opportunities.

The Mega-FTAs and Their Prospects: the TPP, TTIP and RCEP

The acceleration of the development of free trade initiatives has been a phenomenon since the late 1990s. According to WTO statistics, as of October 2016, there are 267 FTAs in force in the globe. While the number of bilateral FTAs has increased, mega FTAs are also in shaping since the 2000s. These mega-FTAs, notably the Trans Pacific Partnership (TPP), the Regional Comprehensive Economic Partnership (RCEP), and the Transatlantic Trade and Investment Partnership (TTIP), not only have significant geo-economic and -political effects but also carry huge implications on the world trade architectures and the rule-making of economic activities in the 21st Century.

The TPP evolved from the Trans-Pacific Strategic Economic Partnership (TPSEP) entering into force in 2005. When the US announced its "Pivot to Asia" strategy, the TPP became the center of US economic engagement in the East Asia. The initiative became strategically important when in November 2009, the US President Barack Obama announced an intention to make TPP an "ambitious, next-generation, Asia-Pacific trade agreement that reflects US economic priorities and values." Since then, the agreement has expanded into the current 12-country[1] mega FTA.

The TPP aims to eliminating all tariff lines and adopts a "negative-list approach" for liberalization in trade in services.[2]TPP's ambition for comprehensive and deep integration is appraised by those countries that prefer FTAs to the WTO. Furthermore, the US participation promises huge market potentials and provides a "buffer zone" for the countries feeling threatened by the rise of Chinese economy. This is the major reason for two ASEAN Member States - Vietnam and Malaysia – to participate in the high standard and comprehensive FTA following Singapore and Brunei.[3] .

On the other hand, at the 19th ASEAN Summit in November 2011, the ASEAN Leaders adopted the ASEAN Framework for Regional Comprehensive Economic Partnership (RCEP). The initiative of the RCEP was soon supported by its six FTA partners, namely China, Korea, Japan, Australia, New Zealand and India. A year later, at the 21st ASEAN Summit, ASEAN Leaders announced commencement of the RCEP negotiations in early 2013. The leaders commit to achieve a "comprehensive, high-quality and mutually beneficial economic partnership agreement establishing an open trade and investment environment in the region to facilitate

1 The 12 negotiating members include Australia, Brunei Darussalam, Canada, Chile, Japan, Malaysia, Mexico, New Zealand, Peru, Singapore, United States, and Vietnam.

2 The negative list approach means that in principle all services sectors shall be liberalized unless specifically excluded.

3 Among them, Singapore and Brunei are the original members in the TPSEP, while Malaysia and Vietnam participated in the negotiations since 2009.

the expansion of regional trade and investment and contribute to global economic growth and development". In May 2013, officials from the 16 governments met in Brunei Darussalam and formally launched the negotiations. ASEAN's decision to develop the RCEP is often perceived as a counter proposal to the TPP as the latter is often regarded as a threat to ASEAN integrity and leadership role in regional economic integration.

ASEAN first aimed at concluding the negotiations by end of 2015 but then postponed to end of 2016. As of August 2016, fourteen rounds of negotiations and two RCEP Ministerial Meetings took place.[4]

The implications of the TPP on the RCEP can be observed in the contents of the RCEP negotiations. First of all, the RCEP claimed originally to set an ambitious goal "to achieve a modern, comprehensive, high-quality and mutually beneficial economic partnership agreement", which is expected to stand to counter TPP's claimed "golden standard" characteristics. Secondly, in the timeline of the development of the RCEP, ASEAN Leaders decided to negotiate the RCEP when TPP accelerated its negotiations. The RCEP initiative was soon supported by its six FTA partners, indicating the intention of ASEAN and its FTA partners to lead economic integration in the region. This also explains why ASEAN has continuously emphasized ASEAN Centrality as a core principle of the RCEP negotiations.

It is important to note that all FTA partners have fully supported the RECP and the ASEAN's centric role. Two reasons for their support are, first, the ASEAN-centric integration process is more politically viable than initiatives proposed by other major powers under current sensitive inter-state relations in the region. Second, although all the FTA partners already have FTAs with ASEAN, including India, the RCEP will improve market access among the 16 countries by further liberalizing trade in services and investment. The RCEP will also liberalize trade between China and Japan and that between China and India, which do not have bilateral FTAs yet and most likely not have one in the next few years. Therefore, the RCEP provides a platform for these countries to enhance economic engagement

4 The 6 rounds of negotiations were held in May 2013 (Brunei), September 2013 (Australia), January 2014 (Malaysia), March 2014 (China), June 2014 (Singapore), and December 2014(India). The 1st and 2nd RCEP Ministerial Meetings were held in August 2013 and August 2014.

under the plurilateral framework.[5] This is indeed RCEP's core values in bring a group of small players and larger economies, including China, Japan and India, into negotiations under extremely complicated geo-political situations.[6]

In the 4th East Asia Summit (EAS) Foreign Ministers' Meeting, the Ministers urged all RCEP participating countries to accelerate progress, as they recognized that RCEP supports and complements the interests of the EAS in contributing to economic integration. Whether the RCEP will reach its goal by end 2016 or first half or 2017 is a test in demonstrating how the region can lead and manage such comprehensive trade negotiations without leadership of large economic powers, such as the US leadership in negotiating the TPP.

However, both the TPP and TTIP are faced with increasing challenges and difficulties outside and inside their countries. After 7 years of negotiations, the TPP was concluded in October, 2015, and signed by its 12 original members in New Zealand in February this year. According to Article 30.5,[7] the TPP shall enter into force either 60 days after the date

5 The RCEP may turn to be an alternative solution for the long awaited China-Japan-Korea FTA, particularly since bilateral relations between China and Japan and between Japan and Korea became problematic over recent island disputes. The RCEP may provide Japan an opportunity to mend its relations with China and negotiate trade liberalization under the plurlateral framework. India is not a party in TPP, APEC or other major regional integration initiatives in the region. India and China also can take advantage of the RCEP as a negotiating forum since two countries completed a joint FTA feasibility study in 2006.

6 Because of the territorial disputes between Japan and China, the proposed China-Japan-Korea FTA has stalled. India and China concluded a bilateral FTA feasibility study in 2006, but has not moved into further action.

7 **Article 30.5: Entry into Force**

1. This Agreement shall enter into force 60 days after the date on which all original signatories have notified the Depositary in writing of the completion of their applicable legal procedures.

2. In the event that not all original signatories have notified the Depositary in writing of the completion of their applicable legal procedures within a period of two years of the date of signature of this Agreement, it shall enter into force 60 days after the expiry of this period if at least six of the original signatories, which together account for at least 85 per cent of the combined gross domestic product of the original signatories in 2013 have notified the

on which all original signatories have notified the Depositary in writing of the completion of their applicable legal procedures, or, in the event that not all original signatories have notified the Depositary the completion of their applicable legal procedures within a period of two years since its signature in February, 2016, it shall enter into force 60 days after 2 years since its signature if at least six of the original signatories, which together account for at least 85 per cent of the combined gross domestic product (GDP) of the 12 signatories (base on 2013 data) have notified completion of their legal procedures. As such, the TPP requires both the US and Japan to complete their ratification procedures at home to satisfy the "6 parties with 85 per cent of the combined GDP" threshold for entry into force of the agreement.

If the US and Japan smoothly ratify the TPP, the earliest time for the agreement to become effective will be April 2018. However, given the upcoming presidential election in the US and unclear situation of whether the new administration will continue to support the TPP and submit for ratification, the TPP may enter into force after April 2018, or even becomes a dead deal in the next few years. If Hillary Clinton is elected as the new President, since the TPP is strategic in maintaining the US interests in Asia Pacific region, it is likely to gain support from her though it may not be "the way it is now", meaning re-negotiation of parts of its provisions may be needed for the new administration to support it.

The RCEP is ASEAN's most important initiative in stepping up further regional integration in East Asia as well as ASEAN's major expression of a global ASEAN. It is largely perceived that both RCEP and TPP can be pathways to East Asian economic integration and the eventual formulation of a Free Trade Area of Asia Pacific (FTAAP).[8] However, if the TPP fails to take effect in 2018, it would be important for all Asia Pacific economies to work together to promote negotiation of the FTAAP, so that the region will

Depositary in writing of the completion of their applicable legal procedures within this period.

8 For example, in 2010 APEC Leaders adopted "Pathway to FTAAP", recognized "FTAAP should be pursued as a comprehensive free trade agreement by developing and building on ongoing regional undertakings, such as ASEAN+3, ASEAN+6, and the Trans-Pacific Partnership, among others". Pathway to FTAAP, Yokohama, Japan, 14 Nov 2010.

continue its path in economic integration and liberalization towards the high standards set forth by the TPP or RCEP negotiations.

On the other hand, if the TPP, the RCEP and the FTAAP co-exist in the future, the overlapping and competing concessions and rules of the different FTAs will make spaghetti bowl effects more acute and significant increase business costs in the region. To solve these problems, efforts will be needed to consolidate or even to promote "multilateralization" of these FTAs.

"Rebalancing"of Economic Integration in the Region -- The role of the Indo-Pacific Region and India

The past two decades have witnessed proliferation of FTAs in Asia Pacific region, thanks to Asia Pacific Economic Cooperation (APEC) and other countries that have taken up pro-liberalization economic and trade policies as a means to open up export markets and promote domestic economic reforms. However, the fact that both TPP and TTIP face with increasing difficulties and uncertainties in the future reflects the "high quality, comprehensive" mega FTAs that aim at solving "behind the borders" issues may not make the FTAs as popular as they were first initiated in the 2000s.

There are a few reasons for the change. First, after several rounds of global trade negotiations initiated by the GATT, average world tariffs have been brought down to a historic low level, in particular in the developed countries. For example, average tariff rates of the US and Europe Union are less than 4 percent, which make the conclusion of the TPP and TTIP less beneficial to European and US merchandise exporters. The TPP and TTIP thus lose their attractiveness to supporters of anti-globalization at home. Secondly, the TPP and TTIP target at "behind the borders" reforms at the counterpart countries, argued by opponents to be "exportation of US-led regulations" and hence increase resistance to them. Thirdly, world economic slowdown and emerging revolution from traditional trade to new forms, such as digital trade, as well as political factors, such as the US Presidential election and the Brexit, an abbreviation of "British exit" from the EU, also affect these FTAs from getting wide support at home.

As such, the economic integration promoted by the major developed country leaders may need a rebalancing. The RCEP, a less ambitious trade deal, is currently more likely. Both China and India are the major players of the RCEP. The RCEP will kick off bilateral liberalization between the two big powers of the developing world for the first time. It has a potential to create significant trade growth and to change the existing production networks and Global Value Chains (GVCs). China and India should work hand in hand to speed up negotiations and conclude the trade negotiations as soon as possible. In addition, India should play a more active role in promoting economic integration in South Asia so that more South Asian countries in Indo Pacific can gradually take part in the world trade and integrate in regional economy. For example, India should encourage more South Asian countries to participate in the RCEP when it is concluded among its original 16 country members and open for new membership.

According to the Guiding Principles, RCEP negotiations are guided by the following major principles: The RCEP will be consistent with the World Trade Organization (WTO), including GATT Article XXIV and GATS Article V;[9] and will, with significant improvements over the existing ASEAN+1FTAs, recognize the individual and diverse circumstances of the participating countries; it will take into consideration the different levels of development of the participating countries, and include appropriate forms of flexibility including provision for special and differential treatment,[10] plus additional flexibility to the least-developed Member States.

The total of RCEP participating countries' combined output in 2013 reached USD 21.3 trillion, accounting for nearly 30 percent of world output. Total trade of RCEP participating countries amounted to USD 10.7 trillion, equal to 29.0 percent of global trade, while total FDI inflows into the 16 countries reached USD 339.8 billion, equal to 23.4 percent of global FDI inflows. If the RCEP can maintain good quality and continue to expand, it can create significant economic benefits to all participating countries.

The increasing importance of the RCEP indicates the need of a "rebalancing of economic integration" in the design and the role the Indo

9 The GATT Article XXIV and GATS Article V stipulate that a Regional Trading Agreement (FTA) should be comprehensive in the coverage of its liberalization of trade in goods and trade in services. GATT Article XXIV sets a "Substantially all the trade" requirement and GATS Article V sets a "Substantial all sectors" requirement.

10 TPP does not have a special and differential treatment provision for less developed members.

Pacific can play. The RCEP, if successfully concluded, may pave way to the creation of a Free Trade Area of Asia Pacific (FTAAP) in the future. The FTAAP will include major powers —China, Japan, the US, and Russia —as well as significant middle players including Australia, South Korea, Indonesia, and other smaller players of the ASEAN countries. The APEC will be the principle institutionalized forum to promote the FTAAP in the next few years.

However, despite of the increased connection between the East Asia and Southeast Asia, there are hardly institutionalized mechanisms or high profile platforms to connect these parts with South Asia and launch talks of economic integration between Indo and Asia Pacific region. Most of all, whether the FTAAP will include India in its future negotiations is not clear yet. Therefore, India should work with like-minded countries and economies to promote such institution-building. It will be an important test to the integration of the Indo and Asia Pacific trade architecture.

Furthermore, free trade itself may or may not create significant employment if, for example, human skills and physical infrastructure are not adequately improved. Thus, the Skill India, Digital India initiated by the Prime Minister Narendra Modi of India, together with his initiatives of the Make in India programs, can be a new showcase of how promoting human skills, improving infrastructure and establishing smart cities can bring new economic growth momentum. In this regard, India should also play a more active role in ensuring effective realization of the Make in India programs and make the programs open for all international partners.

Taiwan's Efforts in Participation in Economic Integration and Response to the Make in India Programs

In the past years, Taiwan has faced with a number of emerging economic factors that are changing the economic landscape. Two of the most important factors are slowdown of Chinese economy and the rise of Southeast and South Asian economy. Since 2010, Taiwan FDI outflows into Mainland China have continuously registered a negative growth, which resulted from the fact that overall investment climate in China becomes less favorable to Taiwanese companies and increasing number of them either chose to close or downsize their operations in China or relocate to neighboring Southeast and South Asian countries, most notably Vietnam and India.

During President Ma Ying-jeou's terms between 2008 and May 2016, in order to participate in regional economic integration, Ma's administration negotiated with China and concluded the Cross Strait Economic Cooperation Framework Agreement (ECFA) in July, 2010, followed by the Cross Strait Investment Agreement and the Services Agreement.[11] In 2013 Taiwan concluded negotiations of an Economic Cooperation agreement (ECA) with New Zealand (Agreement between New Zealand and the Separate Customs Territory of Taiwan, Penghu, Kinmen, and Matsu on Economic Cooperation, ANZTEC)[12], and Singapore (Agreement between Singapore and the Separate Customs Territory of Taiwan, Penghu, Kinmen and Matsu on Economic Partnership, ASTEP)[13], respectively. Both entered into force after ratification.

At regional level, President Ma instructed a "Dual Track" approach to target both the TPP and the RCEP for accession negotiations in the future. Since President Ma announced the government's policy goal to participate in the TPP, a lot of efforts have been made by Ma's administration and continued by the new President Tsai Ing-Wen's administration. Although it is still perceived sometimes by the US that Taiwan is not yet fully ready, the internal atmosphere in Taiwan in the past months has somehow shifted towards a more pro-TPP sentiment. The first reason for this gradual shift is likely benefits the TPP members, particularly Vietnam, will enjoy when the agreement enters into force. The second reason is the continued re-structuring of Chinese economy which means the markets of the US and other TPP countries will carry more weights to Taiwan's external trade now. Further to that, as the TPP requires Taiwan to accelerate economic reforms, it is believed by many pro- liberalization believers that pursuance of TPP will benefit Taiwan in the long term.

11 The Investment Agreement entered into force in Feb 2013, but the Services Agreement was not yet ratified by the legislature.

12 The Agreement was signed on July 10, 2013 and entered into force on December 1, 2013.

13 The Agreement was signed on November 7, 2013 and entered into force on April 29, 2014.

Since 2013, Taiwan government has launched comprehensive regulatory reviews across ministries to identify gaps between existing legislations and the TPP norms, using the text and concessions of the KORUS as a reference benchmark. After February 2016 when the official TPP text was released by the USTR, all ministries re-started the exercise by using the final TPP text and annexes.

As of mid-April, the TPP and RCEP Cross Ministerial Task Force led by the executive yuan has held 16 meetings, aiming to conclude the review exercise by end of 2016. A news release by the executive yuan in October indicated that the regulatory gap has been narrowed down to around 8 laws and regulations, including the Patent Law, the Copy Right Law, the Postal Law, and Electronic Communication Law, among others. These laws may conflict with the provisional requirements embedded in TPP's IPR, TBT, Services and Environment Chapters and need further revision. This means that dozens of regulatory gaps identified in earlier reviews have already been revised or improved.

The government also renewed the impact analysis assessment when Taiwan becomes a TPP member and opens up domestic market. Compared with the ECFA impact analysis assessment conducted in 2009, the renewed assessment expands from economic impact to include social, cultural, gender and human rights impact analysis. This very broad-based impact analysis and assessment is the first of its kind published by the government. It is also an important learning process for both the government and the private sector to examine and respond to emerging sensitive issues related to the 21st Century FTAs and economic integration.

It must be noted that, though not a member of the TPP, the concessions and regulations of the agreement have significant legal and economic implications on Taiwan's external trade and investment activities. For example, Vietnam is Taiwan's second largest outbound investment destination, total direct and indirect investment by Taiwanese companies exceed USD 50 billion. Significant increase of FDI outflows from Taiwan to Vietnam after 2008 when Vietnam participated in the TPP negotiations as a member candidate indicates that the TPP membership has made Vietnam a more attractive destination than other ASEAN Member States.

Furthermore, Vietnam, during its negotiations process for the TPP, has agreed to revise its labour laws and related workplace practices. Chapter

19 of the TPP stipulates that all TPP members will adopt and maintain in their laws and practices the fundamental labor rights as recognized by the International Labor Organization (ILO), including freedom of association and the right to collective bargaining; elimination of forced labor; abolition of child labor; and the elimination of employment discrimination. It also includes commitments to passage of laws governing minimum wages, hours of work, and occupational safety and health. Furthermore, all these are fully enforceable and backed up by trade sanctions.

In addition, not only shall the country abide by all TPP provisions after it enforces the agreement, but it also needs to abide by the requirements stipulated in the exchange of ministerial letters between the Minister of Industry and Trade (MOIT) of Vietnam and the Trade Representative of the USTR. The letters were signed on 4th of February, 2016, as a bilateral legal instrument constituting an integral part of Vietnam's obligations under the TPP. The letters consist of a United States-Vietnam Plan for Enhancement of Trade and Labor Relations.[14] It sets out specific negotiated rights and obligations that are only to be adopted between the USA and Vietnam. As such, apart from the obligations stipulated in Chapter 19, Vietnam shall ensure the right of workers to freely form and join a labour union of their choosing and ensure labour unions are able to administer their affairs with autonomy. Other obligations by Vietnam include worker representation in non-unionized workplaces, selection of union officials, least interference in organizational activity, and scope of strikes.

Since 2015, Vietnam has gradually reviewed its labour laws and workplace practices in order to realize its commitments into new legislations. According to a survey by Chung Hua Institution for Economic Research (CIER) in May this year, most Taiwanese companies in Vietnam perceive the new legislations and strengthened enforcement of existing labour laws one of the most important factors that will shape the overall investment climate of the country and impact their management and operations. Most of all, companies in labour intensive sectors such as garments and textiles, footwear and electronics industries have serious concerns, among others, of freedom of workers to establish grassroots labour unions and expansion of scope of strikes. In this regard, the capacity

14 The Plan shall create rights and obligations only as between the Socialist Republic of Viet Nam (Viet Nam) and the United States of America (United States).

building programs provided by the ILO and the USA will play a vital role in assisting Vietnamese government, labour unions, and local and foreign employers to better respond to the new labour laws.

As the case of Vietnam indicates, the TPP, whether after its entry into force or before it takes effect in some members, will not only change the rules of economic activities of its members, but also has a wide-spreading effect on other non-TPP countries, such as Taiwan, and the regional economy. Furthermore, in addition to labour standards as set forth in Chapter 19 of the agreement, the chapters of strengthened intellectual property rights, environmental regulations and e-commerce, among others, will all have a "spill over effect" on the rule making in the region and may encourage non-TPP countries to follow suit in order to maintain their national competitiveness with TPP members. The fact that Thailand and Indonesia recently announced unilateral relaxation of foreign investment restrictions in certain sectors reflects their intention to compete with Vietnam in attracting foreign investment.

Conclusion and the Way Forward

The proliferation of FTAs, in particular the rise of mega FTAs, has led to overlapping trade architecture, notably in the Asia Pacific region. However, the TPP and TTIP face with emerging challenges and difficulties to conclude or enter into force in their major members. Though it is likely that the TPP may still be renegotiated and ratified after 2018 or 2019 and TTIP be renegotiated, the two mega FTAs and their rosy pictures are less popular than they were first initiated in the 2000s. In this regard, the RCEP, where India is a key player, is highly anticipated and expected to "rebalance" the ambitious trade deals led by developed countries. India should play a more active role in balancing of economic integration in the Indo Pacific region to bring more South Asia countries to gradually participate in the regional economic integration and promote institutionalization of connections between East Asia, Southeast Asia and South Asia.

Furthermore, the Skill India, Digital India, including the Smart City projects and the Make in India programs, can bring focus of free trade back to fundamentals such as strengthening human skills and human capital and improvement of physical infrastructure. India should demonstrate the Make in India programs can adequately deliver the fruits of creation of economic growth and employment. India should also ensure the openness nature of the Make in India programs to international partners.

In the past three years, Taiwan has conducted regulatory review exercises to stock take major trade related legislations in order to examine and improve them in accordance with the TPP requirements. Though whether Taiwan will be invited to TPP's next round of new membership negotiations remains unclear at this juncture, Taiwan is preparing for further economic integration. Taiwan also responds actively to the rise of Indo Pacific economy by registering more FDI outflows into India in the past two years, notably it contribution to the gradual rise of ICT and smartphone supply chains in India by Taiwan's Foxconn and other world leading contract manufacturers of ICT products. Taiwan can be an important friend to India to work together under the Make in India programs and welcoming the rise of the Indo Pacific economy.

Confidence Building Measures and Evolution of Security Architecture in the Western Pacific

Maj Gen (Dr) Nguyen Hong Quan

As the second decade of the 21st century gets underway, the world is witnessing a number of profound and comprehensive changes. Peace, stability and cooperation for development have become an inevitable requirement of nations and remain the main stream in the world. This represents an essential opportunity and foundation for the Indo-Pacific region to make joint efforts to build a peaceful and stable environment, which contributes to promoting cooperation and sustainable development for prosperity in the region and the world as a whole.

Apart from advantages and opportunities, the Indo-Pacific region is facing many difficulties and challenges, including increasingly fierce strategic competition between major powers; disputes over natural resources; sovereignty disputes over territories, waters, and islands; and international terrorism. These disputes are on the rise with an increasing scope, frequency, nature, and scale, which may lead to armed conflict. Non-traditional security threats, especially cyberwar, migration, water and food security, energy security, environmental pollution, climate change, drought, salinization, etc., have more devastating consequences for lives and properties than any armed conflict. It should be noted that no matter how powerful a nation, it cannot solve these problems thoroughly alone. Alarmingly, there still exists a trend towards ignorance of international law and recourse to use of force for the solution of international disputes.

Moreover, against the backdrop of globalization, the dramatic developments in modern science and technology, including those in military science and technology, in the Indo-Pacific region are generating growing interdependence between nations and resulting in change in mode of production, relations of production, and everyone's life. This is an inevitable objective tendency.

Due to its geostrategic and geopolitical importance, the Indo-Pacific region continues to be the most dynamic region in the world. Regional countries are making joint efforts to promote connectivity cooperation initiatives which focus on politics, economy, culture, education, and so on. Pacific Ocean and Indian Ocean not only bring about a number of important benefits for littoral states but represent the world's vital Sea Lines of Communication (SLOCs) and the peaceful living and working environment for millions of people the world over.

However, recent developments, especially competition between nations over several territories and waters and ignorance of international law, are exerting a negative influence on regional security environment in terms of freedom of navigation and overflight and maritime security and safety. Against the background of staggered economic growth, these challenges potentially lead to a regional arms race, growth of mistrust, undermine confidence, and affect cooperation process in the region.

In such a context, aspiration for peace, security, and sustainable development in the Indo-Pacific region becomes ever more urgent. More than ever, all nations must make joint efforts, enhance cooperation on the basis of international law, equality and mutual benefit, protect stability, prevent armed conflict, and avoid a zero-sum game.

May I take this opportunity to express my views on regional security architecture to address effectively broader issues in the Indo-Pacific region.

First, we are in favour of a regional dialogue mechanism. This mechanism consists of major powers, which have interests in the region, and member states to discuss issues related to ensuring a sustainable security environment, free of nuclear weapons, without recourse to threat or use of force in international relations, and respect of international law, including the 1982 United Nations Convention on the Law of the Sea (UNCLOS); and make joint efforts to address effectively nontraditional issues such as terrorism, environmental pollution, security and safety of people working at sea, and dispute over natural resources. This mechanism must not contradict established security cooperation mechanisms[1], but support them.

Second, the Indo-Pacific region is rich in natural resources, especially energy, which are indispensable for economic development of nations in the world. This region represents a huge market with half of the world's population. Most of emerging major powers rely on maritime economy such as China, Japan, India, the Republic of Korea, Australia, Indonesia, and so on. Maritime security relates to economic development of not only littoral states, but also of the region and the world as a whole. Therefore, it is necessary to create a mechanism to ensure freedom of navigation and overflight, maritime trade, and a high level of compliance with international law, including UNCLOS.

Third, it is its geoeconomic significance, economic capabilities, military strength, and political dynamics that make the Indo-Pacific region the world's most dynamic region in the forthcoming decades. The region has a population of about 4 billion people, three out of the biggest economies in the world, the largest democracy in the world, nine of ten biggest ports in the world, seven out of ten largest standing armies in the world, five nuclear states in the world, and a total GDP of tens of trillions of dollars in purchasing power parity terms. The Indo-Pacific region has to cope with a series of threats, which range from low-intensity conflict to nuclear race between neighbouring countries. Radicalism and terrorism have flourished throughout the region. Although there are not many territorial and boundary disputes transplanted into the 21st century, these disputes persist throughout the region. Furthermore, our region continues to be haunted by the spectre of nuclear war, missile tests, and proliferation of weapons of mass destruction (WMD). Moreover, social disparity, uneven levels of development, gap between rich and poor, etc., have provided fertile soil for the growth of terrorism and radicalism. International terrorism and radicalism have even chosen this region as "holy land" in the coming decade.

The regional security mechanism should devise measures to tackle protracted mistrust in the past, prevent nuclear arms race and proliferation of WMD, as well as settle satisfactorily territorial disputes and ethnic and

1 The established security cooperation mechanisms include ADMM+, EAS, ARF, SCO, SAARC, ASEAN, APEC, etc.

religious tensions. Countries cannot have double standards on terrorism. We must prevent and reduce the threat of terrorist attacks in order to make the region be the growth engine of the world's economy for the happiness of almost half of the world's population.

Fourth, the Indo-Pacific region has witnessed many wars between small and big nations. Unresolved territorial dispute is a factor that causes instability in the whole region. Many of these disputes may burst into greater conflicts and wars later. Besides, massive military build-up launched by some regional powers and threatening attitude and willingness to use force, especially in conflicts at sea and SLOCs, would lead to bloodshed and stagnant economic growth in the region and the world. The future security architecture in the Indo-Pacific region should be strong and inclusive enough to deter any military build-up, any military alliance, and any willingness to use force in support of unilateral claims from bursting into conflict at sea or on land, resulting in unexpected consequences.

Fifth, recently, the Indo-Pacific region has become the frontline in cyberwar. The identities of "black hat" hackers have not been revealed, but they are said to be state and non-state actors both in the region and beyond. Cyber-attacks would inflict devastating consequences on lives, properties, and societies.

It is important that the regional security architecture need to work out cooperation plans to respond to any emergencies, foil the plots in the early stages, and expose the instigators.

Sixth, as for non-traditional security threats, terrorist groups, piracy, terrorism at sea, illegal arms trade, drug and human trafficking, etc., the regional security architecture should have more effective and robust measures to minimize their impact on territories in the region.

Humanity is facing a number of huge challenges related to water and energy security, mineral depletion, and depletion of other resources. If oil shaped international geopolitics in the 20th century, competition for available water resources would shape many of international relations in the 21st century. What measures should the regional security architecture have to help countries on the lower course of rivers to mitigate their disadvantages due to their unfavourable geological positions? What measures should the regional security architecture have to prevent consequences of excessive military build-up aimed to cope with such reality?

Over the past few years, global warming, ice melting in the Arctic and Antarctic, etc., have plunged residents in the Indo-Pacific region into potential large-scale humanitarian and environmental crises. These issues cannot be ignored by the regional security architecture. They are the factors that would quietly create instability in the region.

Against such a backdrop, we should reconsider the evolving geostrategic environment, its influence on the region as well as on each nation in the region, especially strategic goals of each nation. In the Indo-Pacific region, there is a growing need for resolution of common challenges and formation of a new political-security architecture in order to promote development, prosperity, peace, and stability. That is also the aspiration of people, who wish to share the same destiny.

We, people in the Indo-Pacific region, should endeavor to set up a regional security architecture to strengthen relations with a view to promoting cooperation and establishing partnerships across the region. Therefore, my view at this seminar is to achieve a brighter future for the Indo-Pacific region and international community as a whole.

In the 20th century, Vietnamese people had to suffer from a great deal of sacrifice and losses during the wars. Given the people's will, self-reliance, and resilience and wholehearted support of the international community, Vietnam has risen from the ashes, poverty, and backwardness. National and international unity has become one of our most precious experiences that has a far-reaching impact on Vietnam's foreign policy and guideline and practical actions. After 30 years of renewal, Vietnam has come out of socioeconomic recession and the state of underdevelopment. Today, Vietnam is a middle income country and is boosting industrialization, modernization and international integration. However, there are still a lot of difficulties and challenges ahead, which require Vietnam to continue to bring into play the lesson of unity, make the most of the people's resources and creativeness, take advantage of sympathy and support of international friends, firmly preserve a peaceful environment, speed up the renewal process in a synchronous and inclusive manner, and ensure rapid and sustainable development in Vietnam.

As far as foreign policy is concerned, Vietnam consistently pursues a foreign policy of independence, self-reliance, peace, cooperation and development, diversification and multilateralization of external relations, proactive and active international integration, being ready to be a friend, a reliable partner and a responsible member of the international community. Accordingly, Vietnam attaches importance to consolidating and developing friendship and traditional relations with neighbouring countries, strengthening cooperation relations with major powers, improving the effectiveness of international integration, and fully realizing its international commitments.

Regarding the South China Sea issue, Vietnam's consistent policy is to struggle resolutely and persistently to safeguard firmly national independence, sovereignty, and territorial integrity; resolve disputes by peaceful means, including political, diplomatic, and legal processes on the basis of international law, including UNCLOS; and request parties concerned to strictly realize the Declaration on the Conduct of Parties in the South China Sea (DOC) and enter into substantive negotiations over a draft Code of Conduct (COC).

Concerning regional and international issues, Vietnam has substantial benefits from building the Association of Southeast Asian Nations (ASEAN) and the Indo-Pacific region into prosperous regions and reliable partners, making contributions to preserving peace and stability and improving compliance with international law.

We believe that an effective security cooperation mechanism in the Indo-Pacific region should ensure unity, democracy, unification, compliance with international law, and benefits to people in the region. That is what people in our region are looking forward to.

Security Architecture in the Indian Ocean Region: Way Forward

Dr Christian Wagner

The Indian Ocean is seen as one of the major security hot spots of the 21st century (Kaplan 2010; Mohan 2012). The economic importance of the Indian Ocean for global trade has often been described. Its sea lanes of communication (SLOC) are the blood veins for both developed countries and emerging economies in Asia and the West. But the maritime region between Africa, Asia, and Australia contains a variety of different conventional and non-conventional security challenges (Bouchard, Crumplin 2010). The region is regarded as a theatre for great power rivalries with the presence of the United States navy at Diego Garcia, China's increasing investment in port facilities in littoral states like Myanmar, Bangladesh, Sri Lanka, and Pakistan, and India's rising blue water capabilities. The non-conventional security threats include piracy, especially at the Horn of Africa, that forms a constant threat to the SLOC in the Persian Gulf and the Arab Sea. But other littoral states, for instance in Southeast Asia, are also confronted with piracy in their maritime domain. Moreover, trafficking of drugs, arms, and humans, failed states, environmental degradation and the protection of marine resources are also part of the non-conventional security scenario.

The debate on how to tackle these different security challenges is still in its infant phase. In contrast to East Asia where the debate on security architecture is in full swing, similar discussions are only slowly developing in the Indian Ocean Rim (Rumley, Doyle, Chaturvedi 2012; Brewster 2014; Sakhuja 2015). Moreover, the debate on Indian Ocean security seems to be characterized by a discrepancy between the strategic relevance of the region on the international level and the absence of noticeable security efforts of the littoral states on the regional level.

The article will analyze the prospects and challenges for security architecture in the Indian Ocean with special emphasis on Europe's engagement. The first part will give a short introduction into the debate on security architecture. The second part will look at the existing forms of governance in the Indian Ocean and the littoral states. The third part will give a short overview on different European activities both from the European Union (EU) and its member states.

Security architecture for the Indian Ocean

The debate about security architecture has its origins in the Cold War period. The Conference on Security and Cooperation in Europe (CSCE) that was established with the Helsinki Accords in 1975 is regarded as one of the first successful examples of a security architecture. It encompassed 35 countries from the Western and Eastern bloc which agreed on permanent consultations and confidence-building measures (CBMs) in three different fields: First, military and security issues, second, economic, scientific, as well as technological cooperation, and third, human rights affairs.

This created a network of conferences, workshops, and expert meetings which intensified the collaboration between the two antagonistic blocs. The Stockholm Conference on Security and Confidence Building Measures in 1986 institutionalized military CBMs like exchange of information on military activities, observation of maneuvers and obligatory on-site inspections. After the end of the Cold War, the CSCE was transformed into the Organization for Security and Cooperation in Europe (OSCE). The CSCE is regarded as a successful institution that helped to overcome the tensions of the Cold War by diplomatic means. Its documents and agreements were no international treaties but acted as a framework of norms, procedures, and regulations. These agreements were also not intended to defeat the other side but were used to improve slowly the relations between both ideological blocs in military matters, economic collaboration and people-to-people contacts.

The concept of security architecture has been used in different areas. At present, the debate is most virulent in East and Southeast Asia. In their seminal work, Tow and Taylor have analyzed the prospects and challenges of the concept for the Asian region. For them, security architecture is "an overarching, coherent and comprehensive security structure for a geographically-defined area, which facilitates the resolution of that region's policy concerns and achieves its security objectives" (Tow/Taylor 2010: 96). Although the definition includes some difficulties, for instance what a geographically-defined area should be, it may nevertheless serve as a starting point for the Indian Ocean Rim.

As outlined above, the Indian Ocean Rim is characterized by a more complex mix of security challenges compared to East Asia. On the one hand there are traditional security challenges like the emerging great power rivalry between the United States, China, and India. On the other hand, the littoral states are confronted with a plethora of non-traditional security challenges. This raises the question what forms of governance already exist in the IOR.

Governance in the Indian Ocean

Governance in the Indian Ocean is characterized by a variety of different institutions. First, the region is surrounded by a variety of regional organizations, for instance the South African Development Community (SADC), the African Union (AU), the Gulf Coordination Council (GCC), the South Asian Association for Regional Cooperation (SAARC), the Bay of Bengal Initiative for Multi-Sectoral Technical and Economic Cooperation (BIMSTEC), and the Association of Southeast Asian Nations (ASEAN).

The focus of most regional organizations is the promotion of economic development and trade. Some organizations like ASEAN have always tried to cover security challenges whereas other organizations like SAARC have never been able to do so because of the antagonism between the most important members, India and Pakistan. A common characteristic of these regional organizations is that they are mostly regarded as weak and inefficient, with ASEAN being the exception.

Second, since the early 1980s there were several attempts to set up institutions which focus particularly on the Indian Ocean and not only on its littoral waters. The first attempt was the Indian Ocean Commission (IOC) that was established by Comoros, Mauritius, Madagascar, Seychelles, and France in 1982. France became a member because the island Reunion is a French region. The main focus of the IOC is economic cooperation but also environmental protection and the promotion of marine biodiversity. Moreover, the IOC has always tried to voice the interests and concerns of the island states in international fora. In 1985, the Indian Ocean Marine

Affairs Cooperation Council (IOMAC) was established as a second organization including Indonesia, Kenya, Mauritius, Mozambique, Pakistan, and Sri Lanka. The aim was to intensify the economic, political, and technological collaboration between the member states. In 1997, India, South Africa, Mauritius and Australia took the initiative to establish the Indian Ocean Rim Association for Regional Cooperation (IORARC). In contrast to other regional organizations, the IORARC tried to include the business and academic community from the beginning. But the aspirations to increase trade among the member states could not overcome the many political, economic and bureaucratic hurdles (Wagner 2013). In 2014, a major revision took place when the organization changed its name to Indian Ocean Rim Association (IORA). Moreover, the charter was revised and was expanded to topics of maritime security.

Finally, a different type of maritime institution is the Indian Ocean Naval Symposium (IONS) that was initiated by India in 2008. Its focus is on Defence and security issues and IONS is seen as confidence building measures between the navies of its 35 member states. The IONS has an informal character and offers workshops, conference, and seminars in order to promote open discussions among the participants.

A common feature of all these different institutions is that they are regarded as weak, the focus being on informal processes and most of them facc a lack of resources and capacities. Therefore, the present set of institutions does not seem to be well equipped to handle the different security challenges in the Indian Ocean Rim.

Europe in the Indian Ocean

Europe has always been present in the Indian Ocean. On the one hand, European countries like France still have territories like Reunion and military bases in Djibouti. Formally, Reunion is a region of France and is therefore also a part of the European Union (EU). The United Kingdom has Diego Garcia whose military installations are also used by the United States.

In order to address security challenges like piracy at the Horn of Africa or failed states, the EU has initiated a variety of programs and measures in recent years (Pejsova 2016). In 2008, the EU member states started the Operation Atalanta at the Somali Coast and in the Gulf of

Aden. The mission operated on the resolution 1816 of the United Nation Security Council (UNSC) to provide free navigation and to protect the supplies of the World Food Program. The operation is regarded as a big success because the incidents of piracy could be brought to zero in 2015.

The EU has also supported the implementation of the Djibouti Code of Conduct (DCoC). The code was adopted by 20 countries from the Arab Peninsula and East Africa in 2009. It committed the signatory states to closer cooperation against piracy in accordance with various resolutions of the UNSC. The EU has been supporting the process of implementation in the signatory states together with other regional and international organizations. The EU's Critical Maritime Routes program (CMR) supported the set up of three information sharing centers in Kenya, Tanzania, and Yemen (EU MARSIC). The EU has also been provided a large part of the budget of the Indian Ocean Commission (Pejsova, 2016: 4). In 2013, the EU in cooperation with the United Nations launched the program "Promote Regional Maritime Security in the Eastern and Southern Africa and Western Indian Ocean Region" (MASE) (European Commission 2013). The program intents to increase the overall maritime security by a variety of measures that aims to enhance and strengthen the legal, legislative and infrastructure capacities of the countries in East and Southern Africa and to improve their coordination and exchange. In 2015, the EU started the program "Enhancing Maritime Situational Awareness in the Indian Ocean" (EU CRIMARIO). It aims to enhance the maritime security in the wider Indian Ocean (European Commission 2015). The objective is to connect the countries of East Africa and the small island states with littoral states in South and Southeast Asia. So far, Malaysia and Bangladesh showed an interest to participate in the new initiative (Pejsova 2016: 4).

The Way Ahead: What security architecture for the Indian Ocean?

The Indian Ocean Rim is plagued by a variety of security challenges and hence, it is difficult to think of one security architecture. It is much more likely that the Indian Ocean will see the development of different security arrangements.

It will be easier to establish security arrangements for the non-conventional security threats. Moreover, it may be useful to start a discussion on subsidiarity, i.e. which level is most suited to deal with the specific security concerns in the most effective manner. For instance, is it necessary to deal with piracy in multilateral institutions like IORA or would piracy not better be handled by the already existing (sub-) regional organizations like ASEAN? A division of labor and competences and collaboration between (sub-) regional organizations and multilateral institutions would also strengthen the respective capacities.

The EU will be an important player in the Indian Ocean. But it should be kept in mind that the EU as a security actor is different from its constituent members. The EU is not a hard power actor but puts a stronger emphasis on its soft power. The indication that most existing regional and multilateral organizations in the Indian Ocean Rim are weak and lack resources gives the EU an added value to support the littoral states in their endeavors to tackle their non-conventional security threats. The EU will continue to invest in activities in order to improve capacity building, infrastructure, connectivity, and coordination among the littoral states.

This will also open new opportunities to enhance the collaboration between India and the EU. The SAGAR initiative (Security And Growth for All in the Region) of Prime Minister Modi in 2015 offers a variety of connecting points for cooperation with the EU, for instance in the field of sustainable development or in building multilateral cooperative maritime security.

Cooperation in the field of security has so far hardly worked in EU-India relations. Both sides were heavily engaged in Afghanistan and shared similar goals and objectives but never found on opportunity for closer collaboration in the realm of security. Thus, the Indian Ocean may offer new opportunities to enhance the EU-India relationship with security issues.

References

Bouchard, C. and Crumplin, W. (2010). "Neglected no longer: the Indian Ocean at the forefront of world geopolitics and global geostrategy" In: *Journal of the Indian Ocean Region*, Vol. 6, No. 1, pp. 26-51.

Brewster, D. (2014). "Beyond the 'String of Pearls': is there really a Sino-Indian security dilemma in the Indian Ocean?". In: *Journal of the Indian Ocean Region*,

Vol. 10, No. 2, pp. 133-149.

European Commission (2013). Programme to Promote Regional Maritime Security (MASE). 1 May, 2013. http://ec.europa.eu/europeaid/programme-promote-regional-maritime-security-mase_en Accessed 31.10.16.

European Commission (2015). EU CRIMARIO: Enhancing Maritime Situational Awareness in the Indian Ocean. http://ec.europa.eu/europeaid/eu-crimario-enhancing-maritime-situational-awareness-indian-ocean_en. Accessed 31.10.16.

Kaplan, R. D. (2010). *Monsoon.The Indian Ocean and the Future of American Power*. New York: Random House.

Mohan, R. C. (2012). *SamudraManthan: Sino-Indian Rivalry in the Indo-Pacific.* Washington: Carnegie Endowment for International Peace.

Tow, William T.; Taylor, Brendan (2010). "What is Asian security architecture?" In: *Review of International Studies.* Vol. 36, No. 1 (January), pp. 95-116.

Pejsova, E. (2016). Scrambling for the Indian Ocean. Issue Brief, 4 February. Paris: European Union Institute for Security Studies (EUISS).,

Rumley, D., Doyle, T., Chaturvedi, S. (2012). "Securing" the Indian Ocean? Competing regional security constructions". In: *Journal of the India Ocean Region*, Vol. 8, No. 1, pp. 1-20.

Sakhuja, V. (2015). The Indian Ocean in 2015, Special Report # 167. New Delhi: Institute for Peace and Conflict Studies.

Wagner, C. (2013). "The Indian Ocean Rim - Association for Regional Co-operation (IOR-ARC): the futile quest for regionalism?" In: *Journal of the Indian Ocean Region*, Vol. 9, No. 1, pp. 6-16.

Security Architecture in the Indian Ocean Region: Way Ahead

Cmde Lalit Kapur (Retd)

Before attempting to forecast what the future security architecture in the IOR will look like, it is necessary to understand the security paradigm for which it must be designed. This paper shows IOR security has evolved over the centuries. It contains the following heads:-

- The IOR and its characteristics, geography and history.
- Stakeholders and their interests.
- Security objectives and challenges.
- The way ahead.

IOR Characteristics

The IOR has 37 littoral states and two extra-regional powers with maritime territory. France has the 3rd largest EEZ in the Indian Ocean, after Australia and Indonesia, while Britain is the 10th largest[1]. The littoral, comprising 2.6 billion people or 39 percent of the world's population[2], includes some of the poorest and richest countries on earth. Per capita GDP even in PPP terms of the Comoros, Eritrea, Mozambique and Somalia is below $ 1500; while that of Australia, UAE, Kuwait, Singapore and Qatar is above

1 Data on size of EEZ obtained from https://en.wikipedia.org/wiki/Exclusive_economic_zone

2 Data compiled from The World Factbook, see https://www.cia.gov/library/publications/the-world-factbook/index.html

$ 65000[3]. Littoral nations attained independence only after World War II and have focused more on finding their feet than on ocean security. The extreme poverty, poor governance structures and feeling of exploitation creates a fragile and volatile environment and failing states; leading to conflict, instability, terrorism and piracy.

The Indian Ocean is now a vital highway for international trade. Two thirds of world oil traffic, half of world's container trade and a third of all cargo moving in the world passes through it. 80 percent of this trade is extra-regional: the IOR littoral is thus a resource provider and security consumer, forcing extra-regional navies to be present to defend their interests. The threats to these interests have changed. There is an upsurge of terror, both as a deniable instrument of state policy as well as a tool of the weak. There is a perception of an increasingly aggressive China, even though one should not get carried away by optics. Numerous middle powers have emerged. All have key interests in the Indian Ocean. The definition of security itself has both evolved after UNCLOS. Pax Americana is no longer able to cope with all the challenges it faces.

Regional security challenges can broadly be divided into two groups: those that existed before UNCLOS, and those that arose after. The former include geopolitical competition and resource security and threats such as WMD proliferation, piracy and SLOC security, and terrorism. Response to these is driven by America. But UNCLOS created additional security challenges, including territorial security, climate change, disaster management and the challenges associated with managing sea spaces under national jurisdiction: resource extraction, environmental degradation, illegal fishing, illegal migration, trafficking in drugs, arms and people, and transnational crime. Most IOR nations are not yet able to secure themselves against these threats, but why should the Pax Americana secure the property of these 'independent' nations? It is this dichotomy that highlights the need for pan-oceanic security architecture.

IOR Geography

Continentally, India is an outlier, cut off from the rest of Asia by the Himalayas and Hindukush ranges, backed by adversarial neighbours to the North and West. From an Indian Ocean perspective however, India is

3 GDP (PPP) data obtained from The World Factbook, see https://www.cia.gov/library/publications/the-world-factbook/rankorder/2004rank.html

central. This centrality is geography's gift to India, one that most Indians are unable to comprehend. It has historically enabled India to link the East, comprising today's ASEAN and Asia's Pacific Coast, with the West, beyond Suez. India's wealth attracted European powers into the Indian Ocean, but its centrality made India the jewel in the British crown, from where British power exercised hegemony over the entire ocean littoral. This centrality is even more crucial in today's globalised era where the Indian Ocean is an indispensable connector for trade and hydrocarbon energy is essential for industrial development. In the Indian Ocean, India can be a security provider, facilitator, spectator or obstruction, depending on the vision of its leaders.

The question in Western minds is, can India be incorporated into the existing hegemonic security paradigm? What India and littorals see as one ocean comprises at least four different sub-regions in the Western strategic perspective, comprising the Persian Gulf and Red Sea; the Northern Indian Ocean; South East Asia and the Southern Indian Ocean. The South and East China Seas comprise yet another sub-region in this paradigm. A number of extra-regional facilities, which could support facilities that were earlier available only from bases, have come up in the Indian Ocean. America has facilities in Djibouti, Bahrain, Diego Garcia, Singapore and Australia. China has a string of projected facilities, in Myanmar, Bangladesh, Sri Lanka, Maldives, Pakistan, Djibouti, Seychelles, Kenya, Tanzania and Madagascar. France has facilities at Reunion and Djibouti, while Japan also has a base at Djibouti.

IOR History

Angus Maddison's conclusion that India and China together accounted for more than half the world's GDP till the 16th century would be familiar to most[4]. India's economic strength was based on a substantial agricultural surplus coupled with a skilled work force that produced high quality

4 Angus Maddison was a British economist specialising in quantitative macroeconomic history. He compiled data on evolution of the global economy for over 2000 years, examining the GDP share of Western Europe, China, the Middle East, India and USA. A graphical representation of his work may be seen at https://en.wikipedia.org/wiki/File:1_AD_to_2003_AD_Historical_Trends_in_global_distribution_of_GDP_China_India_Western_Europe_USA_Middle_East.pngFor an overview of Angus Maddison's work, see Gurcharan Das, in "India: How a rich nation became poor and will be rich again", http://gurcharandas.org/rich-nation-poor.

products in demand by the wealthy everywhere, including across the seas. Predictable monsoons and the Indian peninsula eased the problems of navigation, creating a virtual connectivity brought about by cross-sea contacts, causing trade, arts and scholarship to flourish in cities to which merchants travelled from China and Africa, India and Mesopotamia. Pirates were the only perceived threat[5]. The chronicles of Shi Fa Hsein, a Buddhist monk from Sri Lanka who travelled to China in 414 AD, document hazards including pirates in the numerous islands close to trade routes[6]. National jurisdiction, however, extended only up to the coast. In general, the seas occupied only tertiary space in the strategic concerns of rulers. Consequently, there was no attempt to dominate them. So centuries before Hugo Grotius gave the Western world the concept of Mare Liberum in 1609, the Indian Ocean littoral practised it by allowing merchants to trade and navigate freely without requiring anyone's permission. 'Freedom of navigation' was the maritime security paradigm when Vasco da Gama found the sea route to India.

28 years after Vasco da Gama's arrival, Babur defeated Ibrahim Lodi in the First Battle of Panipat[7], founding the Mughal Empire that would dominate India till overthrown by the British. But Mughal roots were in Central Asia, they cared little for the seas. Babur and his successors set in place a continental mindset, in which land power was the only determinant of the nation's strategic, economic, political and social power. This continental mindset continues to dominate strategic thought in the sub-continent even today.

Vasco da Gama and his European successors challenged the prevailing paradigm focussed on continental power and 'Mare Liberum'. Actually, they believed in what was to become the discredited 'Mare Clausum', legitimised by the papal bulls that divided non-Christian lands between

5 Lakshmi Subramanium, "The Forgotten History of Piracy in the Indian Ocean, Oxford University Press, see http://blog.oup.com/2016/06/history-piracy-indian-ocean/

6 Robert C Beckman, Carl Grundy-Warr and Vivian L Forbes, in "Acts of Piracy in the Malacca and Singapore Straits", edited Clive Schofield, published by International Boundaries Research Unit, University of Durham, UK, 1994, P1

7 Rickard, J (15 May 2010), *First battle of Panipat, 21 April 1526* , http://www.historyofwar.org/articles/battles_panipat_first.html

Spain and Portugal[8]. France, Holland and England were technically barred from trading with or colonising these lands, but engaged successfully in privateering and piracy to contest Portuguese domination of the Indian Ocean, as well as Spanish control over the Pacific. Even the three challengers wished the seas opened only for themselves: the desires of people indigenous to the IOR didn't figure in their thoughts. Over time, superior Western maritime technology shifted regional strategic power from the continental to the maritime domain, where it has remained ever since. It began the era of globalisation which was spurred by subsequent technological advances, which provided other means of connectivity and shrank the world. It led to flowering of the strategy of 'divide and rule', which will always enable maritime power to dominate continental power: unlike the latter, maritime power has no faultlines that an opponent can exploit.

It is interesting to see the stages in transition from a free sea to one where what constituted security was determined by a European hegemon. Amongst the first targets was control of trade and access to the seas. Jockeying among European powers for such controlled to virtually the entire Asian rim coming under their rule, which then spread inland and encompassed all of the Indian sub-continent, while leading to what is now perceived as the Century of Humiliation for the other major Asiatic power. The impact of colonial maritime power was to destroy the ability of the littoral people to use the seas for trade, in turn fragmenting their collective littoral identity on the basis of which colonial power ruled. It broke intra-regional connectivity and regional cohesion, impoverished the people and changed the pattern of trade flow. This change has still not reversed, even though the colonial age ended after World War II.

The massive destabilisation of regional society caused by European rulers forced littoral people to develop new strategies for resistance. Many indigenous people saw the colonial rulers as outlaws and pirates who enslaved them, made unjust laws, extorted money from seafarers for allowing them to venture out to sea and were in large measure responsible for the miseries of society. Indigenous opposition would eventually

8 For an impact of the papal bulls, see VinieRotondaro, "Disastrous Doctrine had Papal Roots", published by National Catholic Reporter, 04 September 2015, see https://www.ncronline.org/news/peace-justice/disastrous-doctrine-had-papal-roots

coalesce into independence movements that would drive out European power from Asia in the post-World War II period. The emergence of USA as a global power led to Pax Britannica being replaced by Pax Americana. The jurisdiction of the nations that emerged, however, extended only up to the three mile limit. Control over maritime spaces remained with first Britain and then America, allowing them to maintain their stranglehold over the Indian Ocean littoral's resources without the politically sordid task of subjugating indigenous people on land.

The Cold War led to geopolitical rivalry and balance of power politics dominating the world. The Indian Ocean was peripheral: American security lay in preventing the emergence of any challenger in continental America while controlling the Pacific and Atlantic to ensure no other power could ever reach them. In the Indian Ocean, new national identities flowered, but Cold War competition and alliances prevented emergence of a collective Ocean identity. With littoral maritime capacity grossly underdeveloped, USA both defined and provided ocean security. UNCLOS substantially expanded national jurisdiction over the sea space, requiring the creation of national capability to govern this space, but regional nations lacked both the vision and the resources required. An IOR effort to recreate the regional connectivity imperial power had begun with the Indian Ocean Rim Initiative in 1995, leading to founding of IORARC in 1997. This has now become IORA. But even today, 16 littoral nations are not members of IORA[9]. It will take a lot of doing to get all on board.

The world is still in the grips of a Pax Americana, which enables USA to dominate the economic, political and security order of the world, including the Indo-Pacific. Regional peace is maintained by American military power, preferably in coalition with likeminded nations, but unilaterally if that is not possible. In this America defined paradigm, all nations can be divided into three categories: the security threats, security consumers and security providers. The overwhelming majority of IOR nations remain security consumers. Those who challenge American pre-eminence are defined as threats, while those who help in maintaining this paradigm, either allies or partners, are defined as security providers.

9 For a list of members of IORA, see http://www.iora.net/about-us/membership.aspx

Stakeholders and Interests

Different stakeholders in the IOR have different interests. The dominant power is USA, for which the drivers are preserving its pre-eminence and the global security order it has created; ensuring access to Middle East energy and for the war on terror; Diego Garcia; freedom of navigation and the security of its citizens and allies. China is the emerging challenger, with somewhat similar interests, looking to push back American power and perhaps establish a PaxSinica, first in the South China Sea and later in the Indian Ocean. Great Britain and France both have territorial as well as resource and trade interests, apart from preserving their status as big powers. Japan and the Asian tigers have resource and trade interests, including security of their SLOCs passing through the Indian Ocean. Littoral focus is on security and development, governance of their maritime areas, unfettered flow of maritime trade, regaining some sort of control over their own destiny and management of the vast maritime commons. But barring a few, littoral slack the maritime capability required.

Security Objectives and Challenges

It is in this environment that a visible aspiration for a cooperative security paradigm, instead of a hegemonic one, has appeared. What does this mean for an IOR security architecture? A mutual security architecture needs a mutually acceptable aim. There seems to be consensus about securing and strengthening the connectivity and upholding freedom of navigation that is vital not only for littoral economies, but also for extra-territorial powers. This translates into ensuring security of SLOCs and air routes, as well as upholding freedom of navigation, although freedom of navigation can mean different things to different people. The need is to create a representative structure that has prescriptive, preventive and enforcement mechanisms: prescriptive to set out common security policies that maximise affinities of geography and culture at least cost while avoiding inevitable local disputes disrupting the common Indian Ocean agenda; preventive to deter wrong-doers; enforcement to apprehend those who are not deterred and bring them to justice. There is little agreement about who will hold the controlling levers of this structure, who will pay for it and how much of a voice should security consumers have, vis-á-vis those who provide security. IOR nations may not be able to pay the necessary costs, but they do aspire to greater control over the functioning of the structure.

Balancing the interests of security providers and consumers is not easy, which is why we had India's Foreign Secretary asking, "How do we address the challenges of connectivity, economy, security, politics, culture and identity, all of which are critical elements to the emergence of a collective Indian Ocean security architecture?"[10]

Even though we all accept that it is inevitable, bringing about change is always difficult. Nicolo Machiavelli had said, "And it ought to be remembered that there is nothing more difficult to take in hand, more perilous to conduct, or more uncertain in its success, than to take the lead in the introduction of a new order of things"[11]. He went on to add, "Because the innovator has for enemies all those who have done well under the old conditions and lukewarm defenders in those who may do well under the new". Let me quote Thucydides, in the Melian Dialogue, circa 416 BC. In it, the Athenian envoy says, "Right, as the world goes, is only in question between equals in power, while the strong do what they can and the weak suffer as they must"[12]. Essentially, notions of morality, Karma or afterlife justice don't figure in the prevailing paradigm of international relations: the world bows only to the strong, who do as they please, while the weak struggle to stay afloat bove the rising tides of history. Some would even quote India's epic, Tulsidas's Ramayana, which says "Samrathkonahi dosh gosain, Ravi Pavak Sursarikinai". The meaning ascribed to these words is that nothing is ever the fault of the powerful, who are like the sun, wind or the Ganges. This interpretation forgets that the Ramayan itself is about the perfect human being; that Indian belief is that only one who is above petty human considerations, somewhat like the Sun, the wind or the Ganges, is fit to exercise power.

Some broad lessons emerge from our survey of the past. First, to paraphrase words used recently by C Raja Mohan in a different context,

10 Remarks by Foreign Secretary at Indian Ocean Conference, 01 September 2016, see http://www.mea.gov.in/Speeches-Statements.htm?dtl/27356/Remarks_by_Foreign_Secretary_at_Indian_Ocean_Conference_September_01_2016

11 Nicolo Machiavelli in "The Prince", Chapter VI, accessed from http://www.constitution.org/mac/prince06.htm

12 Thucydides, in "History of the Peloponnesian War", Chapter XVII, accessed from https://www.mtholyoke.edu/acad/intrel/melian.htm

the principle of power trumps the power of principle[13].The free-riders who want a voice would do well to remember this. Next, history tells us that there will always be need for balance of power to prevent domination by a not so benign hegemon. Third, extra-regional monopoly over the security system leads to colonialism. Such a monopoly will face challenges, particularly as the economic and maritime capacity of regional nations expands. Next, there is the historically proven and undeniable fact that freedom of political and economic choice must be underwritten by the freedom to exercise that choice. This last freedom is what security is all about. Dreaming of political and economic freedom without providing for security is at best wishful thinking, at worst criminal folly. Since security must be provided for, it is vital that all stakeholders get together to determine which security paradigm to put in place. And finally, a veto wielding UN Security Council type model which is hamstrung by geopolitical competition may not be the best security model for the IOR. On the other hand, a democratic construct that gives equal voice to all and works only on the basis of consensus, like the IORA, is unlikely to serve the purpose. We will eventually have to decide on something in between.

The Way Ahead

Looking ahead, my view is that the best option would be to strengthen the IORA while removing its conceptual limitations, instead of trying to create a new construct. The focus of the new security architecture must be limited to maritime security, preferably to the challenges that have arisen after UNCLOS. The future security paradigm for the IOR must cater for a multi-polar world and region. It must be evolutionary and incremental and not revolutionary. It must accommodate the interests of all stakeholders. It must ensure their familiarisation with each other and a mechanism to dispel doubt, while guarding against domination by an elite few. Will such a security construct be achieved? Time will tell.

13 C Raja Mohan, in "Raja Mandala: Power and Principle:, published by The Indian Express, 18 October 2016, see http://indianexpress.com/article/opinion/columns/brics-summit-goa-china-xi-jinping-narendra-modi-pakistan-terrorism-nuclear-suppliers-group-raja-mandala-power-and-principle-3088437/

Valedictory Address

Lt Gen PK Singh, PVSM, AVSM (Retd), Director USI

The Indo-Pacific region contains the largest democracy, the largest authoritarian state, status quo powers, revisionist powers, economic giants, almost all nuclear powers, traditional as well as non-traditional security challenges. It becomes difficult to choose and fit all of them into a seminar, whose length is over a day or day and half.

In our preparation for the event, we looked closely as to why the world is taking note of this particular region. Since the region exists in a wider canvas, we decided to focus on the Indian Ocean and parts of Pacific Ocean, from the Strait of Hormuz to Japan. The seminar has had participants in the past from the US, United Kingdom, Italy and Australia who discussed their views on this theme. We also looked at the Indian perspective and have been successful in raising issues of concern in this region. However, we felt that we were focusing too much on hard military issues in the past and non-traditional issues like blue economy, cyber security and terrorism were being left out. So we picked up those challenges and decided to talk about them. We also believe that in the Indo-Pacific region, it is not only the maritime challenges which are important but meshing them into national security issues of particular countries are important to make the discourse meaningful.

Whatever is happening in the South China Sea and East China Sea has affected the ASEAN as well. Many articles today highlight lack of unity in the ASEAN and that issue deserved focus as well. In terms of regional groupings, how to integrate multiple groups like SAARC, ASEAN and the SCO, engaged us deeply. The shape of future security architecture was of equal interest to us. Would it emerge in continuum of the old, or emerge afresh with little to do with the old organizations? Such follow on issues from this seminar will be discussed in the future. We have been trying to glean the European Union's interests in the Indo-Pacific region. We are happy that Dr Wagner expressed his views on the issue in this seminar.

The happenings in the Indo-Pacific will have a global impact and therefore global powers will be interested in what is happening here. Since nobody will leave this critical geopolitical space out of their focus, there is a need for consistent dialogues like this to constantly evaluate the dynamic situation. We believe this region is intrinsically inclusive and therefore welcomes whoever thinks they have a stake here and can bring peace and enhance coordination through understanding of mutual concerns.

The strategic competition among the big powers in the region has always been there, however it was muted. We pretended it is not there talking only about economy, knowing that a day will come and we will have to talk about strategic competition among the big powers. That day has now arrived as we hedge and rebalance now. My personal view is that India has arrived and has a major role to play in the region. This leads us to the question if it is time for the middle powers in Asia-Pacific to play a more active role. Collectively, they have the power to shape a peaceful future which individually; they may not be able to. Hence, there has to be a common search at what we should collectively be done.

As far as economic challenges are concerned, India is ready to partner anybody and we will not let the minor differences hinder our collective growth. We believe that there is great scope for interaction and partnership keeping differences aside, working towards a win-win situation. What hinders that process is the lack of trust which will develop when we talk more frankly. A platform like this seminar helps in developing trust as we are questioning, and thereby understanding each other better in frank and friendly environment.

The second session of this seminar very aptly looked at the economic aspects and we all know that everything hinges on economy. An interesting point has been made by our Chinese delegate that the budget available for modernization of PLA will not forever be the same and a day will come when high military spending will flatten out as it happens to all countries. In the session on economy we tried to bring emerging areas like the blue economy, geopolitics of energy resources and regional economic integration. The previous seminars were not including these sessions and we have made a beginning. On the security architecture, there is a need to deliberate how we make the structure more effective, if somebody breaks the rules. It's not an easy process as some issues will get resolved bilaterally, some trilaterally and some multilaterally. The challenge of making and defining rules will be always remain.

In the end, I would like to thank all the participants of the seminar. We have learnt so much from your participation and your willingness to share knowledge with us. We hope that many of you would be here next time as well. I also thank the panellists and the audience who have actively contributed to the success of this seminar. You could send us your views as to what else we can include in this annual seminar. We will be delighted to take your views as that is how a conference evolves!

With these proceedings in print, USI National Seminar comes to its logical end.

Concluding Remarks

Maj Gen BK Sharma, AVSM, SM (Retd), Deputy Director (Research), USI**

Any good seminar begins with a good vision. The credit for that vision must go to the USI council and our Director, who selected the topic. When this topic was picked up, it was the recognition of the fact that Indo Pacific is at the centre of gravity of global power shift. This global power shift is characterised by strategic brinkmanship by a 'rising power' and a relatively 'declining power'. That posited a security insecurity dilemma between the two main contenders with other powers trying to align and realign.

When we looked at it in the run up to the seminar, we saw two possible outcomes which we wanted to validate. Following the trend line, one outcome was that we are heading from an era of Cold War to a cold peace. We asked ourselves if that was a desired scenario, and if not what should be the desired scenario? That alternate scenario, we felt, should be one of interconnected zones of collaborative security and co-prosperity. The sense of the house, derived after the seminar, is that we want sustainable peace and co-prosperity. The way to work that out has emerged in an indirect way as managing three '***C's*** with three '*M*'s. The three 'C's being *conflict, competition* and *cooperation* and the three M's being *minimise* conflict, *manage* the competition and *maximise* the cooperation. Therefore any conceptual frame works, architectures and mechanisms will have to devolve around this basic theme, taking incremental steps to develop strategic trust and nudge this strategic space in a positive direction.

The nerve centre of this whole ideation was the Centre for Strategic Studies and Simulation (CS3) where a small team consisting of Group Captain Sharad Tiwari and Dr Roshan Khanijo and other scholars who painstakingly worked the concept note and on the program of work seeking political clearances, networking with all of participants, ensuring that this seminar takes shape. Gratitude is also due to the eminent panellists who travelled long distances from foreign countries injecting flesh and blood into this whole event whose skeletons were created at CS3. I thank you for sharing with us your very rich prospective and cross fertilising ideas which has given certain pathways to follow. My special thanks goes to the vibrant audience especially the dedicated USI members and representatives from the Service Headquarters. In fact, but for a very active audience, we cannot bring in the dynamism to any seminar. That dynamism was manifest in the manner in which they raised questions, shared their perspectives and opinions which encouraged us all. My thanks to my senior colleague Maj Gen PJS Sandhu who helped us reach out with members through numerous mails. I express my gratitude also to the invisible hands of Maj Gen P Goswami, Deputy Director Administration and team who networked everything handling venue management, accommodation, social events, and logistics. He stayed in the background and yet coordinated everything. Thanks are also due to our Director, for inspiration, judicious guidance and plenty of latitude that he gave us in putting this seminar together. With these words, I wish our participants an intellectually stimulating interregnum between our seminars and very happy reading of the proceedings. Your presence encourages us to organise this more efficiently.